INTERNATIONAL SOCIALISM ★

A quarterly journal of socialist theory

Autumn 1

Conten

GW00725865

Issue 72 of INTERNATIONAL SOCIALISM, quarterly journal of the Socialist Workers Party (Britain)

Published September 1996
Copyright © International Socialism
Distribution/subscriptions: International Socialism,
PO Box 82, London E3
American distribution: B de Boer, 113 East Center St, Nutley,
New Jersey 07110
Subscriptions and back copies: PO Box 16085, Chicago,
Illinois 60616
Editorial and production: 0171 538 1626/0171 538 0538
Sales and subscriptions: 0171 538 5821
American sales: 312 665 7337

ISBN 1 898876 19 3

Printed by BPCC Wheatons Ltd, Exeter, England
Typeset by East End Offset, London E3

Cover design by Megan Trudell and Hannah Dee

For details of back copies see the end pages of this book

Subscription rates for one year (four issues) are:

Britain and overseas (surface):	individual	£14 ($30)
	institutional	£25
Air speeded supplement:	North America	nil
	Europe/South America	£2
	elsewhere	£4

Note to contributors

The deadline for articles intended for issue 75 of
International Socialism is 1 December 1996.

All contributions should be double spaced with wide margins.
Please submit two copies. If you write your contribution
using a computer, please also supply a disk, together with
details of the computer and programme used.

INTERNATIONAL SOCIALISM ★

A quarterly journal of socialist theory

TONY BLAIR's march to the right in double quick time has provoked unprecedented pre-election discontent, and not just among the party's rank and file. Alex Callinicos examines all the most recent policy shifts, concentrating on Labour's economic programme. He concludes that although Blair once identified with the kind of revived Keynsianism typified by Will Hutton's bestseller *The State We're In* he is now aligned more closely with the most naked forms of capitalist accumulation.

JAPAN'S ECONOMY is touted as a model by Blair's supporters. But, as Susan Cockerill and Colin Sparks demonstrate, that country's economic miracle is fading faster than at any time in the post-war period.

RICHARD LEVINS is a biologist best known for co-authoring the highly praised book, *The Dialectical Biologist*. He founded Science for Vietnam and Science for the People in the United States. He refused nomination to the National Academy of Science in the early 1970s because of that organisation's role as an adviser to the government's war effort in Vietnam. This year he was awarded the 1996 Edinburgh Medal at the Edinburgh International Science Festival. His address to the festival, 'When science fails us', is a critique of establishment science and a vindication of a dialectical approach to science.

THE BICENTENARY of Babeuf's 'Conspiracy of Equals' during the great French Revolution allows us to examine a moment that has occupied an uncertain place in the annals of revolutionary history. Was it a hopeless act of a desperate minority? Was Babeuf's organisation the forerunner of the Leninist party? Ian Birchall offers a fresh view of an old controversy.

CHRISTOPHER HILL'S new book, *Liberty Against the Law*, is reviewed by Brian Manning, and Paul O'Flinn contributes a discussion of William Morris's *News From Nowhere*.

BOOKWATCH looks at the Middle East peace process and the fate of the Palestinians.

Editor: John Rees, Assistant Editors: Alex Callinicos, Chris Harman, John Molyneux, Lindsey German, Colin Sparks, Mike Gonzalez, Peter Morgan, Gill Hubbard, Mike Haynes, Judy Cox, Adrian Budd, Ian Goodyer, Mark O'Brien and Rob Hoveman.

Betrayal and discontent: Labour under Blair

ALEX CALLINICOS

To say that since becoming leader of the Labour Party in July 1994 Tony Blair has taken the party markedly to the right is to utter one of the commonplaces of contemporary British politics. His first initiative—forcing through the replacement of the commitment in Clause Four of the party constitution to common ownership of the means of production with an avowal of faith in 'the enterprise of the market and the rigour of competition'—proved only to be the beginning. As it became clear that the crisis of John Major's government was terminal and that Labour was entrenched with a substantial lead over the Tories in the opinion polls, so Blair became more daring in the abandonments of past policy that he forced on the party faithful.[1]

The effect of these policy shifts was, on issue after issue, to diminish the difference between Tory government and Labour opposition to the infinitesimally small. The headline to a *Financial Times* article on New Labour's approach to the National Heath Service—'Labour Sets Out to Make Similar Look Different'—could serve to sum up the party's overall stance.[2]

Indeed, on some issues, Blair's team took positions which allowed some Tories to posture as standing to their left. Thus in the John Smith Memorial Lecture delivered in April 1996, Gordon Brown, Shadow Chancellor of the Exchequer, announced that Labour was seriously considering scrapping child benefit for the mothers of 16 to 18 year olds. The £700 million estimated saving produced by this cut would be used, he claimed, to help children from poor families stay on in education after the age of 16. The justification for this policy shift was that child benefit, like all universal benefits, goes to well off as well as poor households. According to the *Financial Times*, 'Mr Blair believes it is invidious that high-income families should receive the benefit...without paying any tax.' Brown attacked child benefit as 'a subsidy for the school fees of the wealthy'.

This move was immediately attacked by Kenneth Clarke, Chancellor of the Exchequer and one of the few surviving representatives of the old Tory left in an increasingly rabidly Thatcherite Conservative Party:

> *I do find child benefit for 16 to 18 year olds the most extraordinary place to go to raid for money to finance things that are supposed to be helping youth training. Just to take away child benefit for that age, with nothing to replace it, hits the average person with teenage children who decide to stay on in education... Another 560 quid [in child benefit] isn't too bad for someone who's sending their child to Eton. Unfortunately, it's 560 quid for the person on below-average earnings whose child just happens to want to stay on at school or college.[3]*

When Blair chose, for fear of the tabloids' wrath, to trail along sheepishly behind Major's absurd declaration of a 'beef war' with the European Union over the BSE crisis, *Financial Times* columnist John Plender commented sardonically:

> *The wisdom of 19th century Whigs on the duty of the opposition could, according to Lord Derby, be summed up cynically and simply: oppose everything and propose nothing. After a week in which Labour has signally failed to offer a clear-cut alternative to the Tories' banana republic diplomacy in Europe, that minimalist view seems to have achieved a new degree of refinement: oppose everything, apart from anything tricky.[4]*

Philip Stephens, another columnist on the same paper, explained Blair's approach in the light of his preparations for actually being in government:

> *His strategy is simple, drawn from the charge that Tony Benn once laid against Neil Kinnock. Get your betrayals in early. The policy shifts of the past 18 months have been calculated to soothe the anxieties of Middle Britain. But they have a second aim. By the time Mr Blair comes to write his manifesto, there will be precious little to betray. He is not waiting for power before confronting the party with its realities.[5]*

No doubt preparing for power underlay New Labour's policy shifts. But those carried through in 1996 had a larger significance in two respects. First, their logic threatened to deprive the Blairite project of the only substantial socio-political content its intellectual backers had given it—the idea of stakeholder capitalism. Secondly, so extreme was the shift to the right that it began to crystallise quite significant opposition to the leadership's drive from within the ranks of Labour itself. I will consider these developments in turn.

The rise and fall of stakeholder capitalism

To say that 1996 marked Blair's abandonment of stakeholder capitalism may appear paradoxical. After all, the year began with him, in a speech of 8 January in that well known haven of liberty and equality, Singapore, promising to create a 'stakeholder economy' where 'all our citizens are part of one nation and get the chance to succeed'. He said:

> It is time that we shift the emphasis in corporate ethos—from the company being merely a vehicle for the capital market, to be traded, bought and sold as a commodity—towards a vision of the company as a community or part- nership in which each employee has a stake and where a company's responsibilities are more clearly delineated.[6]

To understand the idea of a stakeholder economy, and the gap between it and Blair's actual commitments, we must engage in a little intellectual history.[7] Right wing social democracy based itself after the Second World War essentially on the economics of Maynard Keynes. The two classic works of post-war 'revisionism', Anthony Crosland's *The Future of Socialism* and (in a more qualified way) John Strachey's *Contemporary Capitalism* , argued that Keynesian demand management made it possible for the state to secure economic growth, full employ- ment and rising living standards without there being any need to expropriate capital. From the fruits of growth would come the resources needed to eliminate absolute poverty and to reduce social inequality. The revisionists claimed still to be socialists, in the sense that they were com- mitted to the objective of social equality, but they renounced the traditional methods of the left—class struggle and nationalisation—as means for attaining this goal.

Keynesian social democracy flourished during the long boom of the 1950s and 1960s. The faltering and then collapse of that boom in the late 1960s and early 1970s, and a return to class confrontation not just in Britain but throughout the advanced capitalist world, threw the social democratic right into crisis. British politics briefly polarised between the revived classical liberalism of Margaret Thatcher and the hard Labour left under Tony Benn.[8] The Tory electoral triumphs and the defeats suffered by the miners and other groups of workers during the 1980s helped to drive Labour back to the right. But intellectually traditional social democracy was in tatters. Given the apparent failure of Keynesian economics, what plausible strategic vision could Labour now offer?

Under Blair we have seen the acceleration of two ideological trends already under way before he became leader. First, and negatively, there is the definitive abandonment of the belief—central to Keynesian social democracy—that the nation state can manage and regulate capitalism so as to avoid significant market fluctuations. The following declaration by Gordon Brown may stand for many other such pronouncements:

> *World capital markets have eliminated any notion that economic policy can remain a matter solely for national governments… Countries which attempt to run national go-it-alone macro-economic policies based on tax, spend, borrow policies to boost demand, without looking at the ability of the supply side of the economy, are bound these days to be punished by the markets in the form of stiflingly high interest rates and collapsing currencies.*[9]

Globalisation, as it has become fashionable to call it, has thus killed off national economic management. But where does this leave any party committed to reforming capitalism, however modestly? It is here that we come to the second ideological development. The concept of stakeholder capitalism has been used to provide Labour with the strategic vision so desperately needed after the collapse of Keynesian social democracy.[10]

One important source for the concept is provided by the French economist and businessman Michel Albert. His book *Capitalism Against Capitalism* (1991) is to some extent a response to Francis Fukuyama's famous thesis that the collapse of Stalinism marked the end of history in the sense that liberal capitalism no longer faced any rivals capable of offering it a systemic challenge. Fukuyama is wrong, Albert contends, because history will continue as the conflict, no longer between rival social systems, but between different models of capitalism:

> *With the collapse of communism, it is as if a veil has been suddenly lifted from our eyes. Capitalism, we can now see, has two faces, two personalities. The neo-American model is based on individual success and short-term financial gain; the Rhine model, of German pedigree but with strong Japanese connections, emphasises collective success, consensus and long-term concerns. In the last decade or so, it is this Rhine model—unheralded, unsung and lacking even nominal identity papers—that has shown itself to be the more efficient of the two, as well as the more equitable.*[11]

The contrast Albert drew between two versions of capitalism—free market, individualistic Anglo-American capitalism versus regulated, consensual Rhine capitalism—was seized on by intellectuals associated with the Labour right. Of these probably the most important were the journalist Will Hutton, columnist on *The Guardian* and now editor of *The Observer*, and the academic David Marquand, ex-Labour MP and founder of the breakaway Social Democratic Party, but welcomed back into the fold under Blair.[12] It provided them with both the basis of a critique of Tory Britain and an alternative to Thatcher's and Major's policies.

The classic instance of both is provided by Hutton's celebrated bestseller, *The State We're In* (1995). Here he damns Tory policies for reinforcing the long term tendency of British capitalism, under the domination of the City, to pursue short term speculative investment. Any reform of the British economy and state must be in the direction of 'stakeholder, social capitalism', taking as its model the possession by continental European, Japanese and even American societies of 'strong institutions that allow their firms to enjoy some of the gains from co-operation as well as from competition' and which 'are created and legitimised by some broad notion of public or national purpose'. The organised working class, shunned and excluded under the Tories, would find their place in these institutions as, like their German counterparts, 'social partners in the management of capitalism'.[13]

Hutton's call for 'a less degenerate capitalism' is hardly a ringing mobilising slogan.[14] Nevertheless, what Albert claims to be one of the lessons of Rhine capitalism, that 'top economic performance can be wedded to social solidarity through the social market economy', has obvious attractions to social democrats eager to offer reforms without confronting capitalism.[15] Thus, in their 'Dos and Don'ts for Social Democrats', James Cornford and Patricia Hewitt tell their readers:

> Decide what kind of capitalist you are... Social democrats have to do more than recognise market failure when they see it: they have to advance an alternative conception of how market economies should work... The left must construct markets which work by raising standards, not by driving them downwards.[16]

Here, then, was a programme that would allow right wing social democrats to claim that they had a programme with some content, and indeed could offer an alternative to Tory policies. What Gordon Brown calls 'supply side socialism' could square the circle by building a form of capitalism which both achieved a greater degree of social justice and (through investment in 'human capital'—education and training) enhanced the competitiveness of the British economy.

There are three major problems with the idea of stakeholder capitalism. The first is that it seems to be in contradiction to the other ideological shift under Blair—the rejection of any Keynesian strategy of using the power of the nation state to manage the economy. Actually existing stakeholder capitalisms such as Germany and Japan have relied on a high level of state intervention in the economy. Yet consider what Tony Blair said in his 1995 Mais lecture:

> We must recognise that the UK is situated in the middle of an active global market for capital—a market which is less subject to regulation today than for several decades.
>
> An expansionary fiscal or monetary policy that is at odds with other economies in Europe will not be sustained for very long. To that extent the room for manoeuvre of any government in Britain is already heavily circumscribed.[17]

In that lecture Blair committed Labour to 'the control of inflation through a tough macro-economic policy framework'—in other words, he accepted the Thatcherite argument that the priority of government policy is to reduce inflation to a minimum crucially by controlling public spending. UBS chief economist Bill Martin comments: 'Brown, Blair and his economic adviser Derek Scott have chewed, swallowed and digested the central-bankerly proposition that stability is the key to improved economic performance; so much so that Labour's growth strategy comprises little else.'[18]

In their book *The Blair Revolution*, probably the most important single source for understanding real New Labour thinking, as opposed to sympathetic intellectuals' wishful thinking, arch spin doctor Peter Mandelson and Roger Liddle (another SDP renegade welcomed back into the fold) suggest that a Labour government should seek to achieve a stable rate 'for the growth of the value of gross domestic product at current prices—so called nominal GDP'.[19] This policy, justified as a more realistic substitute for the narrow targets for growth in the money supply which the Tories consistently failed to meet in the 1980s, has long been advocated by *Financial Times* columnist Samuel Brittan, one of the chief propagandists for monetarism in Britain.[20]

What Brittan calls 'broad monetarism' doesn't sit well with the interventionism implied by the idea of stakeholder capitalism. It is interesting that Hutton, whose most important intellectual contribution has been to revive Keynes's stress on the pervasive uncertainty endemic in capitalist economies, should have criticised Blair's Mais lecture for its 'underlying assumption that capitalism works best if left to its own devices'.[21] Hutton has also vigorously attacked the closely related 'myth of globalisation'—the idea, in other words, heavily relied on by Blair and Brown, that the internationalisation of capital makes national reforms impossible.[22]

The second difficulty with stakeholder capitalism is really a concrete example of the contradiction just discussed. Quite simply, actually existing stakeholder capitalism is in a lot of trouble. Japan is just beginning to recover from its worst slump since the 1930s, brought on by a frenzy of rather Anglo-Saxon speculation in securities and real estate in the late 1980s, the so called 'bubble economy'. Nor is this merely a matter of past errors which Japanese capitalism has now left behind it. The Sumitomo scandal which became public in June 1996 is a case in point. The huge Japanese trading company announced that it was sacking the head of its copper futures department, Yasuo Hamanaka, for illegal trading that had cost it an estimated \$4 billion. The *Financial Times* described Hamanaka's efforts to control international trade in copper in order successfully to anticipate the movement of copper futures—not the price of the actual commodity but of the 'derivatives' of that price traded on the London Metal Exchange—as part of...

> ...the fashion among Japanese companies for **zaitech**, which was meant to be the use of surplus cash to generate income in the securities markets. What the word came to mean was speculation on a grand scale, incomprehensible to outsiders who characterised corporate Japan as conservative and risk-averse.[23]

Germany meanwhile has experienced extreme cyclical instability over the past few years—the unification boom at the beginning of the 1990s, slump in 1993-4, a brief recovery in 1995 and then back to recession this year. These problems have helped provoke intense debate, in which large sections of German capital have begun to press for drastic reductions in welfare spending, and in the other benefits workers enjoy, in order to enhance competitiveness and profitability.[24]

If the proposed restructuring of 'Rhine capitalism' is successful, the result will be an economy in certain respects closer to the Anglo-American model than it has been in the past. Thus, at the very time when, as we shall see below, Blairite defenders of the Rhine model are proposing changes to British company law to bring it closer into line with that prevailing on the continent, the conservative government of Helmut Kohl is drawing up legislation to allow publicly quoted companies to buy back up to 10 percent of their capital and reward executives with stock options—moves which the *Financial Times* claims 'will help promote the idea of shareholder value in Germany', and thus introduce more of precisely the kind of Anglo-American 'short termism' derided by Hutton and Marquand.[25]

Both the difficulties outlined above point to the same fundamental reality. Stakeholder capitalism in Germany and Japan is just as much a variant of the capitalist mode of production as its Anglo-American counterpart. It is based on the same social and economic inequalities reflecting the exploitation of the working class, and is subject to the same tendencies towards crisis that arise from the nature of capitalism as a system driven by competitive accumulation. The trends described above for German and Japanese capitalism, under the pressures of international competition, to take on some of the characteristics of the more speculative Anglo-American model indicate that the present crisis is one of capitalism as a system rather than of one particular version of that system.[26]

These two problems—the contradiction between state intervention and 'globalisation' and the problems facing the German and Japanese economies—concern the general question of whether or not stakeholding capitalism really is an attractive objective for the working class movement. The third, however, pertains rather to its attractions to Blair and his co-thinkers. As envisaged by Hutton and Marquand at least, the shift to stakeholder capitalism would require considerable institutional changes. These would be of two kinds.

First of all, constitutional reform. Hutton and Marquand subscribe to the interpretation of British history perhaps most influentially developed by Perry Anderson and Tom Nairn, according to which Britain has never achieved a modern capitalist state: the relative decline of British capitalism is, in large part, a consequence of its political domination by a patrician oligarchy closely integrated with the City of London, itself a set of financial institutions characterised by their lack of involvement in industrial investment.[27] Thus Hutton argues that 'the semi-modern nature of the British state is a fundamental cause of Britain's economic and social problems.' Reforming British capitalism therefore requires reforming what Hutton calls 'the semi-feudal state' which presides over it, through the kind of measures advocated by Charter 88—the introduction of a written constitution, proportional representation, and the like.[28]

Secondly, achieving stakeholding capitalism means overhauling British company law. As Marquand explains:

> If the stakeholder concept means anything at all, it means a radical break with the traditions, institutions, and assumptions of Britain's shareholder capitalism. All the manifold varieties of the simple stakeholder model embody the simple proposition that property owners have, and must discharge, obligations to other interests, which also have obligations to them; that the decisions of a capitalist firm must reflect a subtle web of reciprocal obligations, involving its employees, its suppliers and the localities in which it operates, as well as its shareholders. That proposition provides the basis for the sharing of decision rights which are seen as the essence of Rhenish capi-

talism... Either through law, or through the pressure of social convention, the
power-sharing arrangements which lie at the heart of all stakeholder models
are obligatory and enforceable. They have to be: otherwise there is no pro-
tection against free-riders.[29]

Similarly Hutton argues for 'initiatives in corporate governance' to
'break the self perpetuating oligarchy of most British firms... This could
be negotiated initially as a voluntary code, but ultimately it would have
to [be] backed by legislation'.[30] A TUC report on stakeholding calls for
extensive changes in company law to combat 'boardroom greed'.[31]

Introducing proportional representation and reforming 'corporate
governance' are hardly the stuff of revolution. It soon became clear,
however, that even these measures would go much too far for Blair and
his cronies. Thus Blair himself hasn't concealed his opposition to proportional representation, though he still promises to hold a referendum
on electoral reform.[32] Mandelson and Liddle declare: 'We do not believe
that constitutional reform offers the panacea that is sometimes claimed.'
They go on to argue: 'The reform agenda must spring from the voters'
concerns and not follow the master plan of constitutional theorists or be
dictated by the interests of the chattering classes.'[33]

In other words, a Labour government should go in for constitutional
reform only if it proves to be electorally popular. So much for all the
New Labour talk of 'principle' and 'leadership'. Such remarks signal
Blair's intention to weasel out of the various commitments concerning
constitutional reform made by his predecessor, John Smith. Against this
background his retreat in June 1996 from what had seemed to be the
most important of these commitments—devolution for Scotland and
Wales—should come as no surprise. (Rather pathetically, Hutton reacted
to the hullaballoo caused by this reversal with a lengthy piece devoted to
demonstrating the political and economic importance of constitutional
change, but concluded by endorsing Blair's decision to make devolution
conditional on the outcome of referendums in Scotland and Wales
without even mentioning the most direct concession to the Tories—the
commitment to hold a second referendum in Scotland on the proposal to
give the new parliament tax raising powers.)[34]

Though much less publicised, Blair's retreat on stakeholding itself is
more significant because it indicates how little is likely to change under
his premiership. However much it is based on a questionable interpretation of British history and fails to identify the real source of our
problems, the Hutton-Marquand vision of stakeholding capitalism
requires for its implementation a confrontation with entrenched capitalist
interests in the shape of the City and its allies in the Treasury and
company boardrooms. But no sooner had Blair pronounced the phrase
'stakeholder economy' in Singapore in January 1996 than he and his

spin doctors sought to disavow any radical implications it might have. They were particularly eager to dissociate Blair's conception from the detailed proposals for institutional change which Hutton had spelt out in his book. As Noel Thompson writes:

When [TUC general secretary] *John Monks suggested trade unions as the representative institutions through which working people could claim a stake in the management of enterprises and the national economy, the Labour leadership was quick to distance itself from his remarks. Similarly, when John Edmonds of the GMB saw stakeholderism as entailing new legal rights of job security, the response was equally cool. Those, like Will Hutton and David Marquand, who sought to give radical content to the idea...also received a Blairite brush-off. Thus Hutton was categorised dismissively as 'a well-liked, useful, free-thinker, but not a great influence', while Blair himself was quick to rule out the kind of corporate legislation which might give substance to a new vision of corporate responsibilities and behaviour.*[35]

Blair told David Frost that the 'stakeholder economy' was 'a unifying theme or slogan'.[36] Mandelson and Liddle argue that it 'addresses the needs and aspirations of individuals, not interest groups acting for them'.[37] But this is to deprive the concept of stakeholding of any content, since its advocates are concerned precisely to combat what they describe as the 'economic individualism' of the New Right by providing for the representation of interests wider than the shareholders and managers of the company in question in economic decision making.[38]

Mandelson and Liddle nevertheless do argue that a Blair government 'must do whatever it can to promote a stakeholder culture in industry and the City'. They consider the idea of legislation to make company directors 'take into account the full range of interests of those with a stake in a company', but object that:

The danger in any such step is that it would weaken the external discipline that the threat of takeover puts on companies to be efficient and profitable. In other words, it could protect the sleepy at the expense of the thrusting and go-ahead.[39]

Six months after Blair's Singapore speech the *Financial Times* reported, under the headline 'Labour Softens on Stakeholding', that a Labour draft industrial policy document 'fails to live up to the pre-publicity' since it contained 'few specific reforms'. Alasdair Darling, Labour's City spokesperson, told the paper:

There is a limit to how many of Britain's corporate ills can be resolved by leg-

islation. What you are trying to do is change people's behaviour and atti-tudes.[40]

The *Financial Times*, hardly a stronghold of 'Old Labour' thinking, seemed taken aback by the extent of this retreat:

Perhaps most damning is the way that Conservative Party officials admit to being surprised by Labour's decision to try to neutralise the stakeholder issue. They had been concerned that Labour would portray City fund managers as the 'union barons of the 1990s' and attack the government for failing to stop their excesses...

Labour insiders do not deny that it wants to neutralise the stakeholder debate rather than make a virtue of it. The decision stems from the Conservative Party's effective campaign representing stakeholding as a return to the corporatism of the 1970s.

'They are clearly scared rigid of the Tory line and as a result they have bottled what could be an imaginative set of policies,' one Labour official said.[41]

Back to laissez faire

At much the same time David Marquand was sadly drawing much the same conclusion. If Britain is to become a stakeholder economy, he wrote:

...the nettles of institutional design, change and resistance will have to be grasped.

As yet, there is little evidence that New Labour is prepared to do this. It seems to be stuck in the traditional British rut of piecemeal voluntary incre-mentalism, buttressed by a traditional British unwillingness to learn from continental Europe. If it stays there, its noble vision of a stakeholder society, in which all are included, will be nothing but a utopian dream; social inclu-sion combined with economic exclusion is a contradiction in terms. There is still time for it to climb out. But not much.[42]

In early July 1996, amidst a slick media extravaganza, Blair launched his most detailed policy document yet, the *Road to the Manifesto*. The extreme conservatism of this document—its main economic commit-ment was the impeccably Thatcherite assertion that the 'priority must be stable, low-inflation conditions for long-term growth'—seems to have goaded the intellectual architects of stakeholder capitalism into taking something of a stand. Hutton and Marquand joined three other supposed Blairite 'gurus' (the increasingly right wing Christian MP Frank Field, the economist John Kay, and the sometime academic admirer of Mrs Thatcher John Gray) in publishing an article calling for reform of both

'the way the stock market, ownership structures and corporate governance interlock' and 'the institutions of the British state'. This was
supposedly in order 'to construct a more dynamic capitalism as well as a
more cohesive society'. They concluded:

> *Mr Blair and the Labour Party say they should not be interpreted as either*
> *New Right or Old Left, and advocate stakeholding. We agree that this is the*
> *right course. But the programme so far championed falls far short of what is*
> *required. The risk is not in doing too much. Rather it lies in doing too little.*[43]

But it is too simple to see the failure bemoaned by Marquand and
Hutton as simply a consequence of timidity and caution, though these
were undoubtedly factors at work in the retreat from stakeholder capitalism. It was also a matter of the positive preferences of Blair and his
closest allies. Thus Blair on a number of occasions—for example, during
a visit to New York in April 1996—went out of his way to reassure business audiences that his promise to sign up to the Social Chapter of the
Maastricht Treaty (from which John Major secured an exemption for
Britain) would not threaten Britain's 'flexible' labour markets or raise
social costs. In July 1996 he wrote to 10,000 business executives to
assure them that a Labour government would 'insist that any measures
adopted under the Social Chapter promote fairness, not inflexibility. It
will not be used to import foreign social security systems or ways of
organising the boardroom'.[44]

This move represented the effective abandonment of the principal
basis on which the British labour movement had come overwhelmingly
to support the European Community in the late 1980s—the belief that
Brussels could act as a bastion to help protect British workers from the
Tory drive to increase 'flexibility' and cut welfare spending. The fact
that this belief was mistaken does not alter the significance of its implicit
rejection by Blair.

As so often it was left to Peter Mandelson to make explicit the
grounds on which Blair took this stance—the more or less unqualified
endorsement of market capitalism and of the inequalities that unavoid-
ably accompany it. Writing with Roger Liddle, Mandelson declares:

> *New Labour's belief in the dynamic market economy involves recognition that*
> *substantial personal incentives and rewards are necessary in order to*
> *encourage risk-taking and entrepreneurialism. Profit is not a dirty word—*
> *profits are accepted as the motor of private enterprise.*
>
> *Differences in income and personal spending power are the inevitable*
> *consequence of the existence of markets.*[45]

Mandelson was even more explicit in a newspaper article he wrote in April 1996, after completing a tour of the Far East paid for by Barclays Bank in order that he might 'meet many of its Asian corporate customers to talk about trade and investment under a Labour government'. The piece is an extraordinarily crude and unqualified celebration of private enterprise and profit making. Thus Mandelson defends the East Asian boom economies from the charge that they are 'based on sweatshop labour producing cheap, bargain-basement goods, with huge profits and vast wealth for a few being earned through exploitation of the many'.

'Of course,' he declares, 'profits are very substantial and there are some very rich entrepreneurs, but what's wrong with that?' Mandelson pays lip service to the idea of stakeholder capitalism when, for example, he praises the 'conscious attempt by governments such as those in Japan, Korea and Singapore to give their workforce a stake in the country's economic success'. But at the same time he highlights among the 'lessons of Asia-Pacific...an unambiguous commitment to backing entrepreneurial flair—and its rewards—and rejecting the corporatist notion that, by sitting around a table with an agenda of business problems, national representatives of "both sides" of industry can somehow find the solutions'.[46]

Social bargaining between government, big business, and trade union leaders is, of course, a central feature of the Rhine model championed by Hutton and Marquand. Mandelson underlines his rejection of this model by sympathetically quoting a Korean boss's complaint about 'the high costs of the social security system in Germany'. He continues: 'Tony Blair was right in his recent New York speech to rule out the introduction of similar German costs for Britain, an issue, it should be noted, which is quite separate from the social chapter.' In effect Mandelson selects for praise in the East Asian variant of stakeholder capitalism not those aspects stressed by Hutton—the alleged importance of social co-operation in achieving economic efficiency—but rather the unbridled pursuit of profit.

No wonder, then, that one Labour frontbench spokesman on industry, Kim Howells, should appeal to the party: 'Brothers and sisters, embrace competition!' Howells, a former member of the Communist Party, had, as a full time official of the National Union of Mineworkers, played a critical part in engineering the defeat of the 1984-1985 strike. Now he denounced the idea of state intervention in the economy—'Forget the prospect of recreating huge ministries designed to second-guess the markets by favouring one particular sector against another'—and proclaimed the cult of entrepreneurs like the billionaire founder of Microsoft: 'The success of Bill Gates and the crises at IBM and Apple were not determined by Washington's efforts at second-guessing trends in the personal computer markets'.[47] New Labour thinking, at least when practised by the likes of Howells, increasingly resembled such unabashed celebrations of Victorian *laissez faire* as Samuel Smiles's *Self Help*.

'Decide what kind of capitalist you are,' James Cornford and Patricia Hewitt advise social democrats. Tony Blair, Peter Mandelson, and their followers have decided: in the support they have given to more or less unrestrained market capitalism they have opted for what looks suspiciously like the bad old Anglo-American free enterprise model championed by Thatcher and Reagan.

The swell of opposition

Blair's effective gutting of the idea of stakeholder capitalism provides a clear indication of just how conservative his government is likely to be. There are, of course, many others. The former *Financial Times* journalist John Lloyd, an apologist for free market shock therapy in the ex-Stalinist countries, wrote a glowing profile of Gordon Brown in which he attributed to the shadow chancellor 'a political philosophy of vast scope', an attempt at nothing less than 'to redefine socialism'. Under close inspection this 'audacious vision of socialism' turned out to consist of nothing but the replacement of the objective of 'equality of outcome' defended by traditional Croslandite social democrats such as Roy Hattersley with a new goal—'equality of opportunity'.[48]

The only thing audacious about this was the effrontery with which old liberal ideas were being dressed up in New Labour clothes. Hattersley was simply repeating the traditional socialist critique of the essentially bourgeois slogan of equality of opportunity when he pointed out that such equality is meaningless without 'a more equal distribution of power and wealth… A common start to a hurdle race does not provide an equal opportunity of winning if some of the runners are lame'.[49]

To economic conservatism was matched an increasingly ugly tone of social authoritarianism. Blair had first made a public impact when, as shadow home secretary, he effectively took over the new right's case on law and order. Thus, in the aftermath of Jamie Bulger's murder, he said:

> *I have no doubt that the breakdown of law and order is intimately linked to the breakup of a strong sense of community. And the breakup of community in turn is, to a crucial degree, consequent on the breakdown in family life. If we want anything more than a superficial discussion on crime and its causes, we cannot ignore the importance of the family.*[50]

'Family values' have indeed become a dominant theme of New Labour propaganda. Images of vacuously grinning (and all white) families shine from the party's publicity material. The few specific proposals

Blair and his cronies are prepared to make are often directed at families. Thus Mandelson and Liddle suggest 'the provision of medium term, deferred repayment, interest free loans to young couples without access to capital of their own—in effect a form of public dowry, available just once in a lifetime'.[51] And, should families prove to be dysfunctional, then Blair's shadow home secretary, Jack Straw, is there on cue to invoke the power of the state to coerce and punish, as with his call at the beginning of June 1996 for the police to enforce a curfew on youngsters. One of the five specific promises made in Labour's policy document the *Road to the Manifesto* released a month later was 'fast-track punishment for persistent young offenders'.

Straw's outburst helped prompt *The Observer* to protest:

> *Under the guise of left/right arguments having little meaning, New Labour has swerved so sharply to the right that it is in danger of crashing through the central reservation. The presentational spin is that policy should be tough and hard choices made; but the direction of the toughness seems always to involve a concession to the right.*[52]

A few weeks later the same paper listed the systematic retreat Blair had led away from Labour's policy pledges since May 1992. Among the chief abandoned promises were:
- higher rate of income tax no longer to be raised to 50p in the pound;
- pensions to be increased in line with inflation and no longer with rises in earnings (which are usually at a higher rate);
- railways no longer to be renationalised;
- large newspaper groups no longer to be prevented from buying television companies;
- plans for a national training organisation funded by a levy on all but the smallest firms scrapped;
- charter of rights for workers dropped in favour of support for labour market 'flexibility';
- Tory anti-union laws to be kept almost unaltered;
- existing grammar and grant-maintained schools to be retained;
- health trusts now to keep the autonomy granted them by the Tories;
- a ministry of women no longer to be established;
- House of Lords to be reformed rather than abolished;
- Scottish and Welsh devolution now to wait on outcome of referendums.[53]

This last move produced an uproar in the Scottish Labour Party. But the speed of the move to the right—and the unpleasant nature of many of the policies Blair adopted—produced a broader swell of opposition. The most visible form such opposition took was Arthur Scargill's decision, announced in January 1996, formally to break with Labour and to launch a new Socialist Labour Party.[54] This initiative won the support of a small, though significant, number of militants in key manual unions such as the RMT (railways) and CWU (Post Office). It was, however, the tip of the iceberg. Far more trade union and constituency activists than those who followed Scargill out of the party were deeply unhappy about the direction in which Blair's coterie was taking Labour. Thus the 1996 union conference season revealed a degree of criticism of the Labour leadership unprecedented in the run-up to an election. The Fire Brigades Union instructed its executive 'to consider whether Labour represented the interests of firefighters and to look at funding MPs on the basis of whether they stood up for socialist principles or not'.[55] The CWU conference overrode its leaders' opposition to vote for a resolution calling for a Labour government to scrap all anti-union laws.[56] And even the GMB, traditional stronghold of the Labour right, condemned shadow health secretary Harriet Harman for sending her son to a grant maintained school, a decision which 'says quite a lot about her expectations, but very little about ours'.[57]

Resentment against the Blairites was also seething on the Labour back benches. Blair's U-turn over devolution provoked the hitherto ultra-loyal Welsh Labour MP Paul Flynn into denouncing his leadership as 'autocratic' and his policies as 'anaemic'. Flynn described the reaction from Labour activists and MPs:

> I am dealing with hundreds of letters from people who have been in the party for 30 years or more who say: 'We have lost the party.' There is a lot of pain out there; it is almost like a bereavement for some... I have never had so many handshakes from colleagues in the ten years I have been here. And a senior whip came into the smoking room, looked round to make sure no one could see, and gave me a bear-hug. I am far from being alone.[58]

The extent of discontent in the Parliamentary Labour Party led the Blair cabal seriously to canvass the idea of cancelling the 1996 shadow cabinet elections. The 1995 elections had been a disappointment for the Blairites; moreover, Harriet Harman, one of Blair's favourites, was in serious danger of losing her place after the row over her son's schooling. But after over 100 Labour MPs made it known that they were opposed to scrapping the elections, Blair was forced to hold them earlier than normal, in late July. Even the *New Statesman*, reduced under its freshly installed editor Ian Hargreaves to the status of official toady to the Labour leadership, was forced to acknowledge the limits that the affair had revealed to Blair's power:

> In handling the shadow cabinet elections, Blair has behaved in a Major-like

way, not because he wanted to, but because he had to. First, there was the
*compromise: the elections **will** be held, but next week rather than in the*
autumn. Then there were the behind-the-scenes machinations to ensure the
best possible result, including the instruction to those knocking on the shadow
cabinet door not to stand this time.

Is this a foretaste of more regular conflict between Labour MPs and their
leader in government?...enough Labour MPs, including some on the front
bench, have told me that they are keeping quiet until after the [general] *elec-*
tion, but will be speaking out more forcefully afterwards. I suspect many
Labour back-benchers would have insisted on these [shadow cabinet] *elec-*
tions even if the Harman factor had not erupted in January. It is not just a
fluke of a bizarre electoral system that those on the left, from Robin Cook to
Michael Meacher, are always re-elected. They represent a point of view that
will be strong in the PLP after the general election, as it is now.[59]

In the event, Harman kept her place in the shadow cabinet. She only
squeaked in, however, at the very bottom of those elected. Equally significant, at the top of the poll were three women, Margaret Beckett, Ann
Taylor, and Clare Short, all of whom *The Guardian* had reported a few
days earlier were 'detested' by Blair. Gordon Brown dropped from third
to fourteenth place, while Michael Meacher, described as 'utterly
detested', climbed from fifteenth to tenth place.[60] Labour backbenchers
had thus grudgingly gone along with Blair's appeal (backed up by
unprecedented bullying tactics by the whips) to return his existing
shadow cabinet team, but had at the same time registered their protest.

Blair subsequently reshuffled the shadow cabinet in a manner calculated to flaunt his contempt of the poll, notably by demoting Short.
Nevertheless, even Philip Stephens, a journalist very close to the New
Labour clique, who had denounced the affair a week earlier as 'A
Phoney Election', had to concede that 'the return of the same old faces to
the shadow cabinet table was hardly a triumph', and warned: 'The parliamentary party is becoming fractious'.[61] Blair might be getting his
betrayals in early, but the effect was to fuel, at every level of the movement, the kind of anger usually reserved for a Labour leadership that is
actually in office.

Some of the most highly publicised opposition came from unexpected
quarters. Roy Hattersley, for example, played a leading role in attacking
the party leadership's retreat from one of the historic achievements of the
old revisionist Labour right—the introduction of comprehensive education in state schools. Loyal to his hero Crosland, he has also bitterly
opposed the more general intellectual shift to the right, for example, dis-
missing Mandelson's and Liddle's *The Blair Revolution* as 'banal,
pretentious and risibly inadequate'.[62]

Hattersley's transformation from gamekeeper into poacher is an indication of how far this shift had gone. The very attention his criticisms received is also an indication of how muted other voices were. In large part, this reflected the desperate fear that too much internal controversy might deliver the Tories a fifth election victory. Hattersley himself made the point very well:

> Large-scale revolt has been avoided up to now because the Labour Party wants to win. A party leader is like a bank robber who stands in front of the safe displaying the sticks of dynamite that are strapped to his chest. 'Shoot in my direction, and you may cause an explosion that destroys us all.' That tactic can work for a time.[63]

Beneath the surface, however, there are much greater stirrings of discontent. And these affect not just rank and file Labour supporters or even ordinary backbenchers but an important wing of the shadow cabinet. An aspect of Tony Blair's ascent that is strangely ignored by his boosters is his dependence on the Labour's centre left, a group whose members may long ago have shed their links with what was once the Bennite hard left, but which still has important links with the union leaders. The support of his deputy, John Prescott, was, for example, crucial to Blair's easy victory over Clause Four. Prescott's very presence at the top of the party is a reassuring symbol to worried activists of what Labour has not deserted in the rush rightwards. Among the other centre left members of the shadow cabinet is Robin Cook, far and away the ablest figure on Labour's front bench.

There have been a number of tell tale signs that all is not well in the shadow cabinet. Prescott was among a number of members infuriated by Harman's decision to send her son to a highly selective school. Shadow social security secretary Chris Smith led strong opposition to Gordon Brown's proposal to scrap child benefit for 16 and 17 year olds (and so was replaced by Harriet Harman after the 1996 shadow cabinet elections). And Cook carefully worked the trade union circuit, sending out not too subtle signals of his reservations over the Blairite agenda.

Thus a week after Blair had assured New York business leaders that Labour was now a party of the centre, Cook told the Scottish TUC that 'Labour must speak for the poor.' He argued that the 'relationship between the Labour Party and the unions is not a marriage of convenience. It is a recognition of our common commitment to collective action.' Labour and the unions shared two 'core values', community and equality. Though Cook's aides claimed the speech 'entirely accords with what Tony has been saying for a long time', the *Financial Times* suggested that it would be 'welcomed by the left as a challenge' to Blair.[64] At the CWU conference he made what *Socialist Worker* called 'a funny and effective speech' with 'an unspoken but clear message—"You may not trust Tony Blair or Jack Straw but you can rely on people like me and Margaret Beckett".'[65]

Industrial action by workers at London Underground indeed brought the divisions in the shadow cabinet a little more into the open. The Tory government and its press allies sought to use the series of one day tube strikes during the summer of 1996 to embarrass Blair. The London *Evening Standard* carried a full page article demanding that he condemn the strikes. On cue Blair and his shadow education and employment secretary, David Blunkett, reacted by calling for the underground unions to submit their claim to compulsory arbitration. Questioned on BBC Radio 4's *Today* programme on 18 July, Cook pointedly declined the interviewer's invitation to endorse Blair's stand, and merely said that he was bound by the collective responsibility of the shadow cabinet.

These developments are significant because they provide evidence of the fault lines running through the current Labour leadership. When Blair and his team are confronted with the tests of office, over tough and controversial issues such as British participation in a single European currency, these hairline cracks can widen into chasms.

Blair and his immediate coterie are aware that they may not have anything like as easy a ride in office as they have had in opposition. This no doubt is one factor involved in the proposals by Labour general secretary Tom Sawyer to tighten up party discipline, weed out 'below standard or disloyal' backbenchers, and encourage constituency parties to select candidates from a nationally vetted list.[66] After the shadow cabinet elections in July 1996 Blair announced plans to give the whips greater powers to enforce a 'code of conduct' on MPs.[67] These moves are symptomatic of an authoritarian style of party management that goes well beyond anything attempted by Hugh Gaitskell in the 1950s or Neil Kinnock in the 1980s. The influx of new members into the party encouraged Blair to adopt a plebiscitary approach to leadership, in which U-turns are announced without consultation and then ratified by an atomised membership through postal ballots.

Blair's leadership style caused even the generally sympathetic *Financial Times* to write: 'A leader who appears to relish the sobriquets of Lenin and Stalin has bludgeoned those critics who have spoken out against him.'[68] Nevertheless, the extent of the discontent revealed by the shadow cabinet elections led Blair to change tack somewhat and appeal specifically to 'critics on the left', pledging his commitment to 'greater equality' and asking them to 'have faith'.[69]

There is little doubt that, in the longer term, Blair would like to break the link between Labour and the unions. Nic Cohen has written of 'a visceral dislike of trade unionists and, in the words of one member of the

shadow cabinet, a "positive hostility" towards union leaders which no
electoral calculation can explain.'[70] The introduction of state funding of
political parties has been canvassed in New Labour circles as a device
for reducing the party's massive dependence on the unions' financial
support and thus for making a break feasible. But there is an air of unre-
ality about such plans. They would have to gain acceptance, not just
from Blair's own clique, but from the parliamentary leadership as a
whole, including the centre left with their close connections with the
unions. Only an immensely successful government could hope even to
consider undertaking such a difficult and costly enterprise.

But there is not the slightest reason to believe that a Blair government
will enjoy anything that remotely resembles the necessary degree of
success. Bill Martin, City economist of UBS, predicts in an analysis of
such a government's economic prospects that 'Labour would inherit a
large, potentially explosive structural budget deficit' of around 4 to 5
percent of gross domestic product, way above the 3 percent target laid
down by the convergence criteria of the Maastricht Treaty, which Labour
accepts. Reducing this deficit would require 'tax increases or spending
cuts on the scale delivered in the twin [Tory] budgets of 1993: perhaps
equivalent to 7p on income tax rates'. Martin also questions the impact
of the monetary stability promised by New Labour on economic growth:
'From a policy-maker's perspective, the safe assumption is that the pro-
motion of low inflation and a stable cycle would neither impede nor
promote the trend rate of advance'.[71] On the basis of this analysis Martin
suggests that a Blair government was likely to pursue austerity policies:

> Chancellor Clarke, despite his protesting his innocent commitment to sta-
> bility, is not about to wreck the consumer rave now upping the tempo of
> recovery. Faced with an inheritance of more than a year's excess monetary
> growth, Gordon Brown would have little choice but to raise interest rates.
> Indeed, he might press rate rises to the point of overkill in order to demon-
> strate Labour's commitment to economic stability. He would want rapidly to
> acquire the reputation of an Iron Chancellor.[72]

In other words, a New Labour government may find itself confronting
much the same situation as its Old Labour predecessors when they took
office in 1964 and 1974. Faced with the inflationary consequences of
unpopular Tory governments' efforts to hang on to office (the Maudling
'dash for growth' of 1962-1964 and the 'Barber boom' of 1972-1973),
these governments sought to demonstrate their orthodoxy to the financial
markets by demanding 'sacrifices' from their working class supporters—
pay restraint and spending cuts—little different from what they had
experienced under the Tories. Martin is predicting, entirely plausibly,

that Tony Blair and Gordon Brown will react in exactly the same way.

In these circumstances, confrontations between groups of workers and the government are inevitable. The experience of the last Labour administration, which took office in March 1974, and had to face a workers' movement at the peak of its strength, which had just tipped the Tory prime minister, Ted Heath, out of office, is probably not as good a guide to what may happen as events under the Wilson government of 1964-1970. The seafarers' strike of May and June 1966—when a group of workers who dared to defy Labour's incomes policy failed to receive solid support from the rest of the trade union movement and was viciously red baited by the government with the support of the media (especially pro-Labour papers like the *Mirror* and *Guardian*)—probably provides a foretaste of how the Blair government will react to any challenges from below.[73]

Workers' opposition to such a government is most likely to succeed where it is steeled by socialist politics. The more the underlying discontent with Labour's dramatic shift to the right under Blair is translated into an organised socialist response, the harder it will be for a Blair government to get its way. Therefore the months that may separate us from such a government must be spent in active preparation, in the strengthening of socialist organisation independent of both Labour and Labourism.

Notes
1   For more background on and analysis of the Labour Party under Tony Blair, see A Callinicos, *New Labour or Socialism?* (London, 1996) and C Leys, 'The British Labour Party's Transition from Socialism to Capitalism' in L Panitch (ed) *The Socialist Register 1996* (London, 1996).
2   *Financial Times*, 21 May 1996.
3   *Observer*, 12 May 1996.
4   *Financial Times*, 1 June 1996.
5   *Financial Times*, 23 April 1996.
6   *Financial Times*, 9 January and 26 June 1996.
7   See C Harman, 'From Bernstein to Blair', *International Socialism* 67 (1995).
8   For an analysis of this process from a revisionist standpoint, see D Marquand, *The Unprincipled Society* (London, 1988), chs 1-3.
9   Quoted in C Harman, op cit, p28.
10   See, for a useful critical survey, N Thompson, 'Supply-Side Socialism: The Political Economy of New Labour', *New Left Review* 216 (1996).
11   M Albert, *Capitalism Against Capitalism* (London, 1993), pp18-19.
12   The intellectual climate on the new Labour right is well conveyed in the papers (including contributions by Hutton and Marquand) collected together in D Miliband (ed), *Reinventing the Left* (Cambridge, 1994). Hutton calls Marquand's *The Unprincipled Society* 'one of the inspirations behind the concept' of stakeholder capitalism ('Raising the Stakes', *Guardian*, 17 January 1996). Though Marquand does not in this book explicitly distinguish between different capitalist models in the way that Albert does, he makes substantially the same point, arguing that Britain, unlike other major capitalisms, has lacked what Robert Dore calls a 'developmental state': see *The Unprincipled Society*, ch 4.

13   W Hutton, *The State We're In* (London, 1995), pp316, 258, 297.
14   Ibid, p298.
15   M Albert, op cit, p 211.
16   J Cornford and P Hewitt, 'Dos and Don'ts for Social Democrats', in Miliband (ed) op cit, p252.
17   *Financial Times*, 23 May 1995.
18   B Martin, 'So Steady They're Standing Still', *New Statesman*, 19 July 1996.
19   P Mandelson and R Liddle, *The Blair Revolution* (London, 1996), p79.
20   See, for example, S Brittan, *How to End the 'Monetarist' Controversy* (London, 1982).
21   W Hutton, 'By George, This is Not What Labour Needs', *Guardian*, 29 May 1995.
22   W Hutton, 'Myth That Sets The World to Right', *Guardian*, 12 June 1995. A more systematic critique, also from from a reformist point of view, is provided by P Hirst and J Thompson, *Globalisation in Question* (Cambridge, 1996); see C Harman's review of the latter, 'No Place Like Home', *Socialist Review*, May 1996.
23   *Financial Times*, 28 June 1996.
24   See A Callinicos, 'Crisis and Class Struggle in Europe Today', *International Socialism* 63 (1994).
25   *Financial Times*, 16 July 1996.
26   See also C Harman, 'Where Is Capitalism Going?' part I, *International Socialism* 58 (1993), and *Economics of the Madhouse* (London, 1995), pp94-99.
27   See P Anderson, 'Origins of the Present Crisis' and 'The Figures of Descent', both reprinted in *English Questions* (London, 1992). Among the many criticisms of this interpretation of British history, see A Callinicos, 'Exception or Symptom? The British Crisis and the World System', *New Left Review* 169 (1988), and C Barker and D Nicholls (eds), *The Development of British Capitalist Society* (Manchester, 1988).
28   W Hutton, *The State We're In*, ppxi-xii, 323. Hutton's interpretation of British history is scattered throughout his book, but see chs 5 and 11. Marquand offers a more systematic historical account: see D Marquand, op cit, chs 5-7.
29   D Marquand, 'Elusive Visions', *Guardian*, 24 June 1996.
30   W Hutton, 'Time for Labour to Put Some Spine into its Stakeholding Idea', *Guardian*, 22 January 1996.
31   *Financial Times*, 25 July 1996.
32   T Blair interview, *New Statesman*, 5 July 1996. Compare Hutton's explicit call for proportional representation in *The State We're In*, p290.
33   P Mandelson and R Liddle, op cit, pp209, 210.
34   W Hutton, 'It is Broke and It Needs Fixing', *Observer*, 30 June 1996.
35   N Thompson, 'Supply-Side Socialism', op cit, p38.
36   Quoted ibid, p38.
37   P Mandelson and R Liddle, op cit, p25.
38   See, for example, W Hutton et al, 'Tony and the Tories', *Observer*, 7 July 1996. One of the main themes of Marquand's *The Unprincipled Society* is a critique of the individualism he claims is deeply embedded in English culture.
39   P Mandelson and R Liddle, op cit, pp87-8.
40   *Financial Times*, 26 June 1996.
41   Ibid, 26 June 1996.
42   D Marquand, 'Elusive Visions', *Guardian*, 24 June 1996.
43   W Hutton et al, 'Tony and the Tories', op cit, 7 July 1996. Though the next day, with characteristic consistency, Gray was praising the draft manifesto as 'the beginnings of a programme for the modernisation of social democracy' by

'cultivating a new form of capitalism', 'Revival of Reforms', *Guardian*, 8 July 1996.

44   *Financial Times*, 16 July 1996. In a slightly earlier speech Blair also promised that in government he would oppose any extension of majority voting in the EU Council of Ministers to cover Social Chapter employment issues where unanimity is currently required. These include social security, the protection of sacked workers and conditions of employment of third-country nationals.

45   P Mandelson and R Liddle, op cit, p22.

46   *Times*, 23 April 1996.

47   K Howells, 'Industrial Policy', *New Statesman*, 7 June 1996.

48   J Lloyd, 'Iron Will, Steely Intellect', *New Statesman*, 24 May 1996. This piece seems to have been part of a little campaign in the pro-Labour press to raise Brown's profile, which had been a bit blurred both by rumours of his bad relations with Mandelson and by the innuendos directed at his sexual preferences by Sue Lawley in a BBC Radio 4 *Desert Island Discs* interview. Brian Reade, after interviewing Brown, wrote reassuringly, 'You can see how he's a bit of a woman's man. Apart from the brain, he possesses dark, menacing features, a hulking frame and a deep Sean Connery drawl', *Daily Mirror*, 4 June 1996.

49   R Hattersley, 'Bubble 'n' Squeak', *Guardian*, 27 February 1996. See also Hattersley's defence of 'equality of outcome', 'Balance of Power', *Guardian*, 25 July 1996, and Gordon Brown's reply, 'In the Real World', ibid, 2 August, 1996.

50   Quoted in P Mandelson and R Liddle, op cit, p48.

51   Ibid, pp127-128.

52   *Observer*, 2 June 1996. The obscure syntax of the opening sentence suggests the editorial was written by Hutton.

53   Ibid, 30 June 1996.

54   For a discussion of Scargill's move, see A Callinicos, *New Labour or Socialism?*, (London, 1996), pp34-36.

55   *Socialist Worker*, 25 May 1996.

56   Ibid, 15 June 1996.

57   Ibid, 22 June 1996.

58   *Independent on Sunday*, 7 July 1996.

59   S Richards, 'Politics', *New Statesman*, 19 July 1996.

60   *Guardian*, 20 and 25 July 1996.

61   *Financial Times*, 19 and 26 July.

62   R Hattersley, op cit.

63   *Guardian*, 2 July 1996.

64   *Financial Times*, 18 April 1996.

65   *Socialist Worker*, 15 June 1996.

66   *Observer*, 30 June 1996; *Guardian*, 2 July 1996.

67   *Financial Times*, 25 July 1996.

68   *Financial Times*, 1 August 1996.

69   T Blair, 'My Message to the Left: Have Faith', *Independent on Sunday*, 28 July 1996.

70   *Observer*, 28 July 1996. See especially Philip Stephens's piece, clearly based on discussions either with Blair himself or with someone very close to him, in the *Financial Times*, 21 July 1995 (quoted at length in A Callinicos, *New Labour or Socialism?*, p26).

71   *Observer*, 19 May 1996.

72   B Martin, op cit.

73   P Foot, 'The Seamen's Struggle', in R Blackburn and A Cockburn (eds), *The Incompatibles* (Harmondsworth, 1967).

Japan in crisis

SUSAN COCKERILL AND COLIN SPARKS

Introduction

Japan, for so long the wonder of the capitalist world, today displays many of the classic symptoms of economic, political and social crisis.

The country of relentless growth is experiencing something that looks very much like the kind of economic stagnation familiar in other capitalist countries. There are few signs of any return to the years of boom.[1] Just before Christmas the government launched another massive reflationary package designed to kickstart the economy again. The 1996/1997 budget plans to increase government spending and borrowing in order to inject new demand into the economy.[2] The banks face massive bad debts, estimated to amount to 20 percent of the value of the Gross Domestic Product (GDP), accumulated in the wild property speculation of the late 1980s. The 'jusen', the Japanese equivalent of building societies, need a huge bail out from the government to cover their activities during the same period. The proposed budget promises them $US6.6 billion to help solve their bad debt crisis. Nissan, one of the weakest of the big car companies, was forced to close its plant in Zama in April 1995, threatening the entire edifice of 'lifetime employment' in the major companies. The wages and living standards of Japanese workers, which have been transformed beyond all recognition since 1945, are under real pressure today. Toyota, the strongest of the car companies, recently restructured production in its plant in Motomachi: the novelty was that this pioneer of lean and efficient production decided to minimise the use of robots because they were proving more expensive than plain old human beings.[3]

Political life is in chaos. For decades Japan was governed by the Liberal Democratic Party (LDP). This party, very like the Christian Democrats in Italy, owed its origins to the Cold War. A reliable ally of the US, a bastion of the 'emperor system', which has a much greater symbolic importance in sustaining ideas of national identity and history than does the British monarchy, and a loyal friend of Japanese business, one faction or another of the LDP was always able to form the government. This long exercise of power produced the same sort of results as in Italy: politicians became deeply embedded in systematic corruption. At the end of the 1980s, the scale of the scandals became too great and the LDP began to break up. By 1993, for the first time since 1948, Japan had a government headed by a member of the Social Democratic Party. Admittedly, in the years in the wilderness, the party had dropped its opposition to US bases, defence spending, the national anthem and the emperor. In government it depended on the votes of one of the successor parties formed out of the factions of the LDP. Nevertheless, the post-war mould was broken. Since then the recomposition of the party system has proceeded apace. The Social Democratic Party itself is splitting up, with its current leader and former prime minister, Tomuichi Murayama, attempting to form a new 'liberal' party, openly committed to deregulated capitalism.

Socially, the stresses and strains of a capitalist crisis have begun to create ripples on the surface of Japanese society. One of the most assiduously propagated myths about Japan is that it is radically different from other countries. One aspect of the myth of difference is that Japan is an egalitarian society without social classes and with a very low degree of social conflict. Recent events have started to call that belief into question. The Great Hanshin earthquake in and around the industrial city and port of Kobe, which took place in January 1995, was more than just a natural disaster. The response by the authorities was so bumbling and inefficient that thousands suffered needlessly. The image of Japanese society as a smooth functioning machine was wrecked by the incompetence and corruption that were all too obvious. At the same time, the disaster manifestly had a much greater impact on the poor and working class areas, with their relatively flimsy housing, than it did in the richer areas. A year after the disaster 40,000 people, most of them old and poor, were still living in temporary accommodation. Inequality in Japanese society was vividly illustrated in the statistics of death, injury and displacement.

Even more dramatic have been the events following the release in March 1995 of the toxic gas Sarin in the Tokyo underground—11 people died and 4,500 were injured. The subsequent investigations seemed to point to the existence of a large and well organised religious movement, the Aum Supreme Truth, that was so much at odds with official Japan that it was effectively at war with it. In December 1995 the Socialist government launched a legal process to ban the sect. The law they used was the 1952 Subversive Activities Prevention Law.[4] This monument to the Cold War, which the Socialist Party had always denounced in opposition, had previously been used against left wing individuals but never before against an organisation.

Such phenomena are not, of course, direct manifestations of class conflict, but they are certainly evidence of the great internal pressures in a society. These show up in universally recognisable forms. There are, for example, an estimated 10,000 homeless sleeping on the streets of Tokyo. Many are victims of the collapse of small and medium companies in the present recession.[5] They face constant police harassment and an almost total lack of any official support network. If there is little overt social struggle in Japan compared with many capitalist countries, that is because it is strongly repressed rather than because its causes are absent.

Many in Japan perceive there to be a deep and pervading crisis. One commentator wrote in his review of 1995 that:

*To borrow the Latin phrase Queen Elizabeth II used to describe the year 1992 for the British royal family, 1995 for Japan was an **annus horribilis**. Two extraordinary events alone—the 17 January Great Hanshin earthquake, which killed 5,480, and the unending string of bizarre crimes allegedly committed by the Aum Shinrikyo cult—were enough to mark 1995 as a horrible year for the nation. The two combined to make the Japanese people realise that the safe society of which they were so proud could no longer be taken for granted. But there was more to be glum about during the year. On top of the natural and man made disasters were the deepening political chaos and the continuation of the economic slump, both of which were compounded by crises in the nation's financial system. All of these factors added up to a mood of general unrest and concern about the country's future among the general public... Many of the events that beset Japan in 1995 could be attributed to a common theme—the breakdown of the carefully nurtured system that had worked to keep the country moving forward over the past 50 years. Beyond the trouble these events caused on the surface, they forced the nation to address fundamental questions about Japanese society itself. A look at the nation's political situation bluntly exposes the national drift that has occurred over the past few years... The nation's economy also languished throughout the year, although a few signs of weak recovery raised hopes from time to time. Meanwhile, most economists predicted that next year's performance would not be much better. One issue that stood out in the midst of the general*

economic malaise was the crisis in the financial system. A few institutions—
Cosmo Credit Cooperative, Kizu Credit Cooperative and the larger Hyogo
Bank—collapsed in the aftermath of the plunge in real estate and stock
values that left financial institutions with a huge amount of uncollectable
loans, estimated by the government to amount to at least 40 trillion yen...Just
when it seemed that things couldn't get worse, they did. In early November,
American authorities shut down the US operations of Daiwa Bank, Japan's
tenth largest city bank, as punishment for the conducting and covering up of
illegal trading activities at Daiwa's New York branch. That added to distrust,
both at home and abroad, of Japan's financial system and the Ministry of
Finance, which closely oversees the banks.[6]

It is true that the Japanese have always been much less confident
about the all conquering power of their economy than admiring foreign
economists, but there is no doubt that 1995 has seen a new level of doubt
and uncertainty even about the fundamentals of Japanese society.

The shattering of the illusions about Japan has been greeted with
mixed feelings outside of the country. Some right wing commentators,
particularly in the US, have seized on them with joy. For them, all of
these things are evidence that the Japanese model of social cohesion and
strong state intervention is not superior to that of the free market, individualistic model of the US and Britain. For others, particularly the right
of the British Tory party, the consequence has been to shift attention to
the 'Asian tiger' economies. These, it is argued, constitute an even better
model for emulation since they are much more flexible than their giant
neighbour, which must pay the price for its strong state intervention and
increasing use of Keynesian economic policies. For commentators like
this, it is important to emphasise every sign of problems and of social
crisis, for they demonstrate that the end of the Japanese miracle is at
hand.[7]

On the left, or whatever that section of the political spectrum occupied by Tony Blair and the British (New) Labour Party might be, many
of the old illusions remain untroubled. For them, Japanese capitalism is
different to, and better than, its British cousin. Japanese businessmen
understand the need for investing in education and infrastructure.
Japanese companies treat their employees as human beings rather than
mere 'hands'. Japanese business and Japanese politicians reach comfortable agreements about joint policies and pursue them in the long run and
in the national interest. Michael Meacher, for example, wrote in the
aftermath of Tony Blair's tour of the Far East:

Economically, there is no alternative to a close partnership between private
industry, the finance sector and the state, to end the destructive short-termism
of recent years. All the world's most successful economies have developed in

this way. They have also promoted a modern training and education system so that citizens can take advantage of economic opportunities when they arise. Most have also sought a social partnership between employers and employees. The term 'stakeholder economy' captures these objectives very well.[8]

The fear for people like Blair is exactly the reverse of that of the right wing commentators. New Labour wants the old Japan of high growth rates and social peace to re-emerge as a result of the moderately reflationary policies of the government and to continue to place its traditional emphasis on the long term. They hope to emulate those features of Japan and dread that this might not prove a solution to the problems of British capitalism. The aim of this article is to show that both of these perspectives are wrong. Japanese capitalism is indeed in crisis and that crisis will not easily be resolved. It is likely that out of the present turmoil will emerge a country in which there is more, and more obvious, class struggle. But, on the other hand, the end of Japanese capitalism is not nigh. It is most unlikely that the social structures erected over the decades of boom will collapse immediately. Japanese capitalism will remain for the foreseeable future one of the most powerful and robust in the world.

In order to demonstrate the crisis affecting Japan, we need first to look at the origins of the Japanese economic miracle before going on to consider the problems that it has now run into. Against that background, we can look at the state of the Japanese working class and the potential it has for emerging as an independent force capable of challenging the whole system.

The Japanese miracle

Of course, Japan is different. All historical examples of capitalism are different. British capitalism is different from German capitalism. Italian capitalism is different from US capitalism. Argentinian capitalism is different from Indonesian capitalism. The pressures of the world market and the globalisation of capitalism are not yet sufficient to efface these differences of history and of natural comparative advantage. The interesting questions are: how far and in what ways is Japan different? There is a strong train of thought which argues that Japanese society is fundamentally different from other societies, and that Japanese people are radically different from other ethnic groups.[9] Less extreme versions hold that there is a special kind of 'Japanese model' of society which confers competitive advantage on Japan, and which Western ruling classes should emulate in order to be just as successful.

In fact, it is quite possible to understand at least the main features of

Japanese society and the evolution of Japanese capitalism using the standard methods of Marxist analysis. There are certainly differences to be noted and accounted for, but there are also strong similarities with other class societies and with the structure of other capitalist economies. In analysing Japan, a number of the main theoretical developments in Marxism associated with this journal and its predecessors turn out to be absolutely vital. As we shall see, it is impossible to understand either the successes or the problems of Japanese capitalism without an understanding of the complex nature of bourgeois revolutions, the role of the state in the capitalist economy, the impact of arms production on the world economy and its constituent parts, the way in which capitalism can develop unevenly and reach its most advanced forms in very backward countries, and the impact of structural divisions in the labour force on the ability of the working class to defend its own interests and fight capitalism.

There is something real to understand and explain. Between 1950 and 1985 the Japanese GDP grew by 1,409 percent. This contrasted with 557 percent in Western Germany, 323 percent in the US, and 223 percent in the UK.[10] Japanese growth rates during this period were not only very high compared to those of other countries, they were also high in terms of historical comparisons. One leading Marxist Japanese scholar wrote in 1990:

In the 22 years from 1951 the Japanese GDP grew continuously and rapidly by 9.2 percent per annum on average, making it seven times as big as a result. The annual growth rate was elevated from 8.9 percent in 1951-61 to 9.4 percent in 1961-73. These were remarkably high rates of economic growth in historical experience in the world. As a result, in the two decades until 1973, Japanese GNE (Gross National Expenditure) per capita multiplied 12.5 times in nominal yen and 4.9 times in real terms. This process was certainly not merely a quantitative change. In the first half of this period, various home electrical appliances such as cleaners, TVs, washing machines, refrigerators, which had been almost non-existent in Japanese economic life just after the Second World War, became popular and generalised. In the second half, along with the sophistication of these home appliances, an automobile society with a general ownership of cars was constructed.[11]

Japanese capitalism thus not only grew very quickly, but at the same time it transformed the social structure of Japan. In 1950 wage workers made up only 39.3 percent of the total Japanese working population. By 1970 wage workers made up 64.2 percent. In absolute numbers, they had increased from 14.2 million to 33.8 million. The main industries which suffered erosion as a result of this change from independent petit bourgeois production to collective proletarian labour were the primary industries of agriculture, forestry and fishing, and most notably agriculture. The percentage of the employed population working in these industries fell from 54.2 percent of the total in 1947 to 8.3 percent in 1987. In absolute terms, it fell from nearly 18 million to just under 5 million during the same period.[12]

The role of state capital

In order to understand this rapid and protracted growth, we need to take a brief glance at the history of modern Japan. This is usually taken as beginning in 1868, with the overthrow of the Shogunate and the restoration of the power of the Meiji imperial dynasty. There is a huge controversy over whether this constituted a bourgeois revolution or not.[13] For Marxists in the tradition represented by this journal, this is a slightly mistaken debate. The dynamics and character of any revolution are extremely interesting, but the essential issue is not whether a revolution is actually carried out by the bourgeoisie, or even whether its leading proponents believe that they are establishing a bourgeois society. For us, the key question is what kind of social and economic outcomes flow from the revolution. In the case of Japan, it is quite clear that the effect of the Meiji restoration was to enable the flowering of industrial capitalism, and in that sense it fulfilled the main historical functions of a bourgeois revolution.[14]

The kind of capitalism that emerged, however, was deeply marked by the time and place of its origins. The Japanese ruling class embarked upon its industrialisation policy at precisely the moment at which European and US capitalism were entering the most aggressive phase of territorial expansion associated with classical imperialism. Indeed, the coup which overthrew the Shogunate was a direct result of the 'black ships' of the United States navy forcing the Japanese to open their ports to foreign trade. The Japanese ruling class needed to look no further than China to see the fate which awaited the state which could not defend itself against the imperialists.

The section of the ruling class which emerged victorious in the 1870s embarked upon industrial development in much the same spirit as Stalin was to do half a century later in the USSR: it was their intention to develop modern industry in order to equip themselves with modern weapons. In order to retain their ability to rule, they were quite happy to ditch major elements of Japanese tradition and Japanese society. For the outside observer, there could be nothing more 'Japanese' than the samurai. In fact, the Meiji government launched a massive attack on this class and provoked serious opposition:

...samurai opposition initially took the form of armed uprisings that sought to

*topple the government. The underlying cause of the rebellions was profound discontent and considerable economic distress within the former warrior class caused by early Meiji reforms that dismantled the feudal polity and all but abolished samurai elite status... Viewed as the organised, political response of a dispossessed social class, the half dozen **shizoku** rebellions between 1874 and 1877 can be explained as the predictably violent reaction of a traditional elite displaced by a modern revolution.[15]*

In their positive programmes, they consciously modelled some of the major new Japanese institutions on the best available capitalist models. The state bureaucracy and the army were rebuilt on Prussian lines. The navy was constructed as a carbon copy, right down to the details of the uniforms, of the British Royal Navy.

They also recognised that a country coming late to capitalist development needed strong state intervention in order to survive. In fact, the Meiji state itself was the organiser of industrial production in many cases, primarily for military production.[16] The use of tariffs and other protective measures enforced by the state was necessary to protect infant industries from foreign competitors. The toleration, indeed the encouragement, of large scale integrated groupings of companies was necessary to ensure that production was on a sufficient scale to survive. The subordination of the immediate needs of particular companies to a conception of a longer term interest was implicit in the fact that military production was the main aim of industry.

At the same time, unlike in some other later developing capitalisms, the ruling class recognised that they could not industrialise by cutting themselves off from the world market. The country was simply too small and too poor for an autarchic solution to be credible. In the first phase of capitalist development, taking place in the high period of territorial empires, the orientation on the world economy meant trying to construct their own empire to rival the worst European examples.[17] In this, they had some success, notably in defeating Russia in 1905-1906, and establishing colonial rule in Korea. Later, in the 1930s, they invaded China and set up a puppet government in Manchuria while struggling to control as much of the rest of the country as possible.[18]

Thus two major trends which are often held up as examples of the uniquely 'Japanese' nature of capitalism in that country, and explained in terms of the timeless features of the society, are in fact the direct result of the immediate historical circumstances in which industrial capitalism began to develop there. State intervention in industry, going so far as to constitute a powerful tendency towards state capitalism, was recognised as a general feature of the imperialist age by Bukharin.[19] If that recognition took an extreme form in the case of Stalinism in the USSR, the same tendency towards a fusion of state and capital was present in many other economies in the same epoch, and for the same reasons of imperialist rivalry. Japan was, and to some extent still is, an example of just such a general trend.

To argue that the Japanese ruling class saw its interests with a peculiar clarity, and that it pursued them with a ruthless logic, is not to claim that they possessed a degree of insight not given to the capitalists of other countries. They certainly made mistakes. The most notable was the lunatic decision to attack the incomparably superior power of the US. In the long run, such a war could only have one outcome: the defeat of Japanese imperial ambitions.[20]

The permanent arms economy

Military defeat in 1945 had far reaching consequences for Japanese capitalism and launched it on the path which has led to its current position. The most obvious consequence was that it spelt the end of any attempt to play the role of an independent imperialist power: in that sense, the aim of the Meiji restoration had been as unrealisable as the attempt to build socialism in one country. Japan was occupied by the US, which dictated a new constitution and set about 'democratising' Japan in its own image. As we shall see, the internal consequences of this process very rapidly went too far for General MacArthur and President Truman. At the same time, the collapse of the Chang Kai-shek regime in China forced the US to look for a new secure base to fight communism in the Pacific. Japan was the main beneficiary of that new situation.

The world economy in the long post-war boom was dominated by what has been known in this journal as the 'permanent arms economy'.[21] In essence this theory argues that the structural problem facing capitalism is that, as it produces greater and greater amounts of surplus value, so the ratio of machines to workers (called the organic composition of capital, which expresses the relationship of dead to living labour) rises. The result of this is that the rate of profit tends to fall over time and this can only be reversed by the destruction of large amounts of capital. That is normally done by slumps, in which machines and factories stand idle and finished goods decay. It can also be done by wars, in which factories are bombed, warships are sunk, and there is general all round destruction. However, from an economic point of view, the same effect can be achieved simply by devoting substantial resources to military production, without ever fighting a war. Capital and labour expended on weapons production are 'luxury' production which generates no new productive capacity. When the warship or the bomber is obsolete, the exchange value embedded in it is destroyed every bit as much as if it had been blown apart. This portion of the social surplus is thus not available for reinvestment, so the tendency to overaccumulate capital is slowed down, although it is not reversed. The tendency to endemic crisis is thus reduced.[22]

After the end of the Second World War, arms expenditure in the major economies remained at a very high level compared to previous periods in the history of 'peacetime' capitalism. This meant that the system avoided the kind of sharp contractions which had been such an obvious part of the economic life of the 1930s. In the place of regular catastrophic slumps, there was a long boom in capitalist production. There were still the booms and slumps of the standard business cycle, but these did not produce the drastic systemic consequences which had had such a severe effect before the Second World War.

This phenomenon had three major consequences for the development of the Japanese economy. The first of these was the general effect which arms spending had on the world economy as a whole. The general expansion of the economy meant that each part of it could, potentially at least, hope to expand. To the extent that it benefitted from the general improvement in economic conditions as a result of the permanent arms economy, Japan gained the same advantages as did all other western capitalist economies. It is, as Rupert Murdoch will tell you, much easier to enter an expanding market than a contracting one. It was thus relatively easy for what was then a small and backward economy to find niches in world trade which it could occupy and in which it could prosper.

The second advantage gained by Japan was general to the defeated side in the Second World War, although it was particularly strongly felt in Japan. The losers, most notably Germany and Japan, were prevented from full scale re-armament. They were, therefore, in the position of enjoying the benefits of the permanent arms economy without having to pick up the tab. For the system as a whole, the scale of expenditure on armaments was colossal: according to Michael Kidron, in the late 1950s it accounted for 'about one half of gross capital formation throughout the world'.[23] This meant that there was an overall 50 percent reduction of the amount available to capitalists for reinvestment. But the taxation which shifted that surplus out of the productive cycle and into armaments was borne by capitalists in Detroit, Birmingham and Lille. Capitalists in countries with much lower arms expenditure had available to them a relatively greater proportion of the surplus they appropriated for direct productive reinvestment. Both Germany and Japan were in this position. They were prevented by the settlements imposed upon them by the victors of 1945 from developing large military machines. In the case of Germany, this was relaxed in the 1950s as part of the Cold War, when West Germany was permitted to rearm, although not to the same extent as its former enemies. Japan, though, was constitutionally obliged to renounce militarism and this was enshrined in the convention of not spending more than 1 percent of its Gross National Product (GNP) on the 'Japanese Self-Defence Forces'. Although this was in practice often slightly exceeded, it was not formally abandoned as a target until 1989. Thus for decades, when some of the other major Western capitalist economies were putting between 4 and 10 percent of their GNP into what was, in strict economic terms, pure waste, Japanese capitalists were able to reinvest more or less all of their share of the surplus.

The third beneficial effect of the permanent arms economy on Japan was the result of the geography of the Cold War. Two of the main points at which the global struggle between the US and the USSR turned into open warfare were Korea in the early 1950s and Vietnam in the 1960s. In both wars Japan was an important base and staging area for the US and direct US military expenditure produced a massive stimulus to the Japanese economy. The impact of these expenditures was very considerable, and helped to transform the situation of the Japanese economy. A major bourgeois historian of the Japanese economy wrote:

Most economic historians emphasise the enormous influence of the Korean War on Japan's economy at this crucial stage, and it is certainly true that the war triggered an unexpected boom just at the point when the economy was suffering the full impact of the stabilisation panic created by the Dodge Line. The Korean War boom proved to be an unexpected shot in the arm and made it possible for Japan to make a complete economic recovery almost at a single stroke...

The economic boom resulting from the Korean War was the largest and the most important in Japan's post-war economic history. It was triggered by the special procurements income that derived from US army expenditures and by the sudden rise in exports that accompanied the expansion of world trade after June 1950.

Special procurements, or special Korean War demand, may be defined in two ways. Defined narrowly, the term refers to the enormous order for goods and services for the UN forces in Korea placed with Japan in a very short time by the commander of the Eighth Army and by the supplies department of the American army in Japan. This was largely due to the fact that Japan was the industrialised country nearest the war zone and, therefore, the best source of emergency supplies. Even when considered in this narrow sense, foreign currency income from special procurements reached about $1 billion during the three years of the Korean War, about 70 percent and 30 percent for materials and services, respectively... The broad definition of special procurements includes this direct procurement by the UN forces and the yen *expenditure of military personnel stationed in Japan as well as staff of foreign organisations such as relief and aid programs. In the period from 1950 through 1955, special procurements taken in this broad sense are estimated to have reached $2.4 billion to $3.6 billion... The temporary foreign currency income from special procurements amounted to between 60 percent to 70 percent of exports, raising the balance of payments ceiling at a single stroke.*[24]

Combined and uneven development

The shape of the economy that emerged from this distinctive set of circumstances had a number of unique features. Despite the existence of an advanced industrial sector, petty agriculture, handicraft industries and small scale distribution still had the greatest weight in the economy, making up 60 percent of the employed population. Japanese capitalism was thus an example of the juxtaposition of very highly developed large scale capitalist production methods alongside other practices which had not yet left the feudal epoch. The industrial companies which dominated the 'modern' sector of the economy were not only very large, they were also few in number. A few firms dominated the production of major commodities other than food.

Despite their initial zeal for democratisation and demonopolisation, the US occupiers had quickly changed their views when fighting communism became the national religion. The old structure of highly integrated large scale industrial and financial enterprises like Mitsubishi, Mitsui and Sumitomo remained more or less intact: the former *zaibatsu* simply became the new *keiretsu*. There is a very close link between these large conglomerates and the banking system, which provides most of the investment capital. The extent of large companies' dependence on traded equities is generally regarded as still much lower than in Britain or the US. This is one source of the 'long-termism' of Japanese business, which is relatively free of the risk of takeover and able to raise capital without recourse to the stock market.[25]

Partly because of the small size of the modern sector, Japan developed relatively little of the apparatus of the welfare state which is associated with developed capitalism: private savings and family structures filled the gap. As a consequence, levels of personal savings held in long term deposits in Japan were very high compared to other capitalist countries. This remains the case even today. In the decade 1980-1990 savings on average made up a 32 percent share of GDP in Japan as opposed to 17 percent in Britain, 23 percent in Germany and 16 percent in the US.[26] It is this saving, channelled through the banking system, which makes up the funding available for investment.

A divided working class

The extreme differences within the economy meant that there was a large internal reserve army of labour which could be sucked into modern industry during periods of expansion and expelled back onto the land, or into the small family business, during recessions. The automobile industry, which is often taken as the purest form of Japanese capitalism, illustrates the process clearly. The trend for auto manufacturers in the US was to attempt to act as 'vertically integrated' producers, owning plants producing all of the parts needed for the production process. In Japan, on the other hand, the major car makers subcontracted large parts of production to outside companies. These 'second and third tier' companies, which often had their employees working in the car assembly plant itself alongside regular workers, were much smaller in size and provided nothing like the same stability of employment, wages and conditions as Toyota or Nissan.[27]

As we shall see, the structure of industry in Japan is such that the famous 'lifetime employment' policy is the preserve only of a relatively small proportion of workers in the largest companies. The wage differential between workers in large companies and smaller companies is also much higher than it is in other economies. According to one estimate, for companies with between 50 and 99 employees, wages in Japan were 58 percent of those in companies with more than 1,000 employees in the 1980s, as compared with 74 percent in Germany.[28] As one Japanese economic historian remarked:

> *Actually, the Japanese labour market was lax throughout the 1950s and 1960s, through having both a plentiful rural latent surplus population in agricultural families, and a surplus stagnant urban population in small and often family businesses. On the basis of such a surplus population, a dual structure of wages and working conditions between big business and small business was formed and much utilised by the former through the subcontracting system. It must be obvious that the greatest contributing factor for the rapid rise of Japanese economic growth was the favourable conditions in the labour market for firms and the resulting relatively cheap labour in comparison with rising productivity or with labour costs in other advanced capitalist countries.[29]*

One direct result of this kind of employment structure is that, in combination with a weakly organised working class, it enables rises in real wages to be kept low relative to productivity gains. Over the 30 years from 1955 to 1985 productivity in Japanese manufacturing rose 1,112 percent, while real wages rose by 360 percent.[30] The competitive advantage such a situation permits can be grasped by means of international comparison. In the decade 1975-1985 Japanese productivity rose by 217 percent while real wages rose by 106 percent. In the US the comparable figures were 134 percent and a fall of 1 percent. In Britain there were rises of 132 percent and 102 percent. For Germany, the figures are 135 percent and 113 percent.[31]

The end of the great boom

Despite these four areas of difference, however, Japanese capitalism remains very clearly a variety of the normal private capitalist model. It is true that the rate of growth has been high, but Japan has displayed the same business cycle characteristic of such economies. These phases of expansion and contraction are much more evident to the Japanese than they are to the casual outside observer. There are even special names for the different events. Thus 1957 saw the 'Jimmu boom', 1958 saw the 'bottom of the pot recession' and 1961 saw the 'Iwato boom'. The great boom of the late 1980s is known as the 'bubble economy'.

The other obvious tendency which Japanese capitalism shares with other countries is that, as the economy matures, the explosive growth rates vanish and are replaced by an expansion closer to the international norms. In the 1960s the annual average rate of GDP growth in Japan was 10.9 percent as opposed to 4.1 in the US. In the 1970s it was 5 percent as opposed to 2.8 in the US. In the 1980s it was 4.1 percent as opposed to 2.7 in the US.[32] These converging growth rates are one important index of the fact that Japanese capitalism has begun to shed its apparently unique features and resemble more obviously the international norm for an advanced capitalist country. The nature of the current recession is another important piece of evidence.

In considering the contemporary problems of the Japanese economy we have to start from the fact that the mechanisms which played such an important role in its initial successes 45 years ago have had a progressively smaller impact on the world economy for the last 20 years. The long boom was over by the mid-1970s. It has been replaced by a period of booms and slumps which, while not yet historical calamities as in the past, have certainly been much more marked than in the immediate postwar period.

The proportion of the world product spent on arms had been on a downward trend since the end of the Korean War. There was a reversal during the Reagan years, but the end of the Cold War has meant a dramatic fall in expenditure. The overall effect of the process on the world economy has thus been reduced. Japan's own expenditure has been growing. Although today it is, in absolute terms, the second largest in the world, it is still only a small proportion of a very large GDP.

Nevertheless, its growth does mean that Japanese capitalists are now bearing more of the direct costs of armaments production than they were in the past. There has been no new hot war on Japan's borders to provide an extraordinary stimulus to demand, as the Korean and Vietnam wars did. All three of the advantages that Japan enjoyed as a result of the permanent arms economy thus started to evaporate in the mid-1970s and are of less importance each year.

Secondly, the very success of the advanced industrial sector in Japan meant that it slowly eroded the reserve army of workers on the land and in petty production. At the same time, there has been a rise in the proportion of women entering the workforce, to the current level of 41 percent of the total.[33] One consequence of this is that there has been a shift from the older reliance upon family structures as the main supplier of social security towards formal public provision. As a consequence, social security expenditure as a proportion of the GNP rose from 4.6 percent in 1970 to 10.3 percent in 1980 and has continued to rise ever since.[34] The fact that the vast bulk of production in Japan is now fully capitalist means that the overall level of wages is much higher than it was in the past, and compares in real terms with the wage levels elsewhere in advanced capitalism. The comparative advantage conferred by low wages outside of the industrial sectors has passed from Japan to the other 'Asian tiger' economies of the region.

The third major change which has undermined the vitality of Japanese capital is the increased importance of the world market. This has had three effects on Japan. In the first place, there has been increasing international controversy about Japanese trading practices. While the modern capitalist sectors of the economy were always internationally oriented, they in fact constituted a relatively small part of Japanese production. Up to the 1970s Japanese capitalism existed within the relatively protected bounds of the state. One direct consequence of this is that Japan has always run a substantial balance of payments surplus. As Japan has become more and more a major force in the world economy, the capitalists of other countries, particularly those of the US, began to demand an end to the 'unfair' protection that their rivals enjoyed. Japan began to abandon formal protection in the 1970s and 'by 1977, Japan only had 27 items on its tariff lists, 22 of them being agricultural products'.[35] Subsequently the Japanese government has entered the familiar process of deregulating, privatising and 'liberalising' the economy.

The process has been a slow one, and there are still major points of friction between Japan and its trading partners, particularly the US and the European Union (EU). These often focus on so called 'invisible' trade barriers which prevent Western firms competing on the same terms as their Japanese rivals in the internal market. Sometimes this is nonsense. The US government complains that the Japanese do not buy US cars. Apart from the fact that quite a lot of Americans prefer Japanese cars, there is an obvious and very visible trade barrier which has nothing whatever to do with protectionism. The Japanese, like the British, drive on the left. The Americans drive on the right. With the exception of two models, US car companies do not produce right hand drive models for sale in Japan. The two right hand drive models sell fairly well, but overall US cars only account for 3 percent of total Japanese sales. Cars produced in the EU, 200 models of which are available with right hand drive, make up 5.8 percent of the Japanese market.[36] Japanese companies, of course, produce left hand drive models for the US market. It is true that there are some other areas of trade in which there do appear to be some obstacles to imports to Japan, but overall the trend in Japan is very much towards removing trade barriers. In the trade disputes which still take place, it is not at all clear that Japan is always the obstacle to free trade.[37]

This relaxation of state controls and intervention reduces the ability of the state to sustain that close relationship with big industry which has been such a continuing feature of Japanese economic life.[38] Japan is not alone in finding that the increasingly global scale of the world economy makes it difficult to continue with the classic state capitalist remedies.

Secondly, the continuing trade surplus has meant that there has been a steady appreciation of the value of the yen, particularly relative to the US dollar. From around 240 to the dollar in 1985, the yen today stands at around 100, and at one point on 19 April 1995 it was as high as 79.75. The US is the largest Japanese export market and the expansion and contraction of the Japanese economy are closely related to the business cycle in the US. Just as in Britain, the sharp boom of the later 1980s, which apparently solved the economic problems of the earlier years of the decade, took place on the back of the 'military Keynesianism' of the Reagan years. Adverse exchange rate movements relative to the US dollar are thus extremely serious for Japanese industry. This currency appreciation has placed enormous pressures on Japanese capitalism to remain competitive by cutting costs and raising productivity. In this they have been very successful. Despite the fact that the yen has risen from around 240 to the US dollar in 1985 to about 100 now, Japan continues to enjoy a substantial trade surplus with the US.

The third major effect ties together the consequences of the first two. The result of loosening the close link between state and industry and allowing greater play to the unregulated market is that the movement of capital has itself become internationalised. In the first place, this means that Japan has become a major exporter of capital in its pure money form. The US budget deficit of the 1980s and 1990s has largely been financed

by Japanese capitalism's willingness to buy US Treasury bonds. It has'
also meant that Japanese industry has increasingly invested abroad in
plant and machinery, at first in the US and Europe and today in the rest of
Asia. Although the Japanese economy is coming to play a central role in
South East Asia, it remains true that the US and, to a lesser extent, Europe
are still the most important places for both export and investment.[39]

This productive investment has immediate advantages for Japanese
capitalism in that it bypasses some of the criticisms of Japanese trading
practices, and some of the defensive barriers put in place against
Japanese import penetration. The investment in developing countries
also has the massive advantage that it is in countries which today enjoy
the sort of advantages accruing from the uneven development and low
wages which Japan itself possessed in an earlier period.[40] In the case of
plants in Asia, the goods produced are often imported back into Japan.
The major disadvantage is that this process of 'hollowing out' threatens
both the relationship of Japanese companies with their home workforce
and their relationship with the Japanese state itself.

As a result of all these internationalising factors, it is far more difficult today for the Japanese government to find the means to restart the
boom. The aftermath of the financial crisis brought on by the classical
processes of speculation in property and the stock exchange in the late
1980s has been to worsen what was already a recognisable response to
the patterns of the world economy. It is against this background that the
future of Japanese capitalism has to be seen.

The Japanese working class

The fourth major factor in the current situation facing Japanese capitalism is the nature of the workforce at its disposal. It is, after all,
Japanese workers who have made these phenomenal production gains
possible and who actually make the very high quality goods for which
Japan is famous. It is here that the heart of bourgeois mystification about
Japan is to be found. It is argued by outside observers of both right and
left, not to mention by many Japanese themselves, that it is in the special
nature of Japanese society, the Japanese family, and the Japanese worker
that the real key to the success of the country is to be found. Workers in
other countries might be alienated: the Japanese love their company and
its products. Workers in other countries might skive: the Japanese love to
work. Workers in other countries might complain and take industrial
action: the Japanese are passive and docile. 'If only,' you can almost
here the outside observers saying, 'If only we could distil those attitudes,
bottle them and slip them into the canteen tea at home.'

This myth does rest on an element of truth. Japanese workers are very productive and very flexible. The working methods in Japanese factories are the most efficient in the world and they have been emulated more or less successfully by every capitalist anywhere who even thinks about competing on the world market. There is relatively little open class conflict in Japan, few official strikes and even fewer unofficial ones. The mythic nature of the account lies first in supposing that the working methods are uniquely Japanese and secondly in believing that there has always been a high level of passivity amongst Japanese workers.

The first of these is easily dealt with. In fact, parts of the panoply of production methods associated with Toyota and claimed as uniquely Japanese — quality circles, absence of status differentials, etc — were dreamt up by a US industrial relations expert, William Deming. Ignored in his home country, his ideas about involving workers in production decisions in order to ensure quality and efficiency were taken up enthusiastically in Japan. When he died in 1995, his death was more remarked on there than in the US. It would be wrong to fall for another myth about Japan and claim that these methods were all imported and that therefore this is just more evidence of the uncreative nature of the Japanese compared to Westerners. In fact, the methods were taken up and improved in Japan and the key innovation which is today so admired, 'just in time' production, was a uniquely Japanese contribution to capitalism, largely devised by Ono Taiichi.[41] Like most other advances in capitalism, indeed in the history of humanity, Japanese production methods represent a development of ideas germinated elsewhere and mixed with an original local contribution.

The alleged passivity of the Japanese working class is another myth, but requires slightly greater attention. Like every other working class in the world, the Japanese working class has had its periods of activity and victory and its periods of passivity and defeat. The distinctive feature is that the defeat at the end of the last great outburst of militancy had much more drastic and long lasting consequences than did similar setbacks in other countries.

Trade unions, socialism and communism all made early appearances in Japan.[42] As was to be expected in a country in which the military elite retained a central place in the political system, they experienced extremely severe repression. An upsurge of militancy following the First World War was crushed and the history of the 1920s and 1930s is one of terrible repression.[43] Immediately before and during the Second World War workers were forced into semi-fascist corporate 'unions' similar to those in Italy and Germany. The working class was comprehensively atomised. This did not mean that they were happy. As Garon puts it:

Deprived of their own organisations, the demoralised workers protested in the only ways possible—absenteeism, job switching, slowed production, and the manufacture of defective goods. Worried police noted numerous cases of disputes or 'near disputes' in the final years of the war.[44]

The US came to Japan with the slogan of 'democratisation', and Japanese workers believed them. SCAP dissolved the corporate body (Sampo) set up by the military, and General MacArthur told prime minister Shidera that he expected them to encourage 'the unionisation of labour'.[45] They launched a phase of what is now known in some circles as 'overenthusiastic democratisation'. In 1945 just 3 percent of Japanese workers were in trade unions. Twelve months later 46 percent were members. By 1949 this had reached a peak of 56 percent. There was an enormous strike wave. Factories were occupied. Journalists and printers took over bourgeois papers. Demonstrators tried to break into the imperial palace in Tokyo. Soviet type organisations appeared in one or two places.[46]

Faced with this massive unrest, the US occupation authorities, who had 400,000 troops in the country, changed their position. They dropped their opposition to the old imperial order and announced that they would intervene to 'preserve order'. On 31 January 1947 General MacArthur personally issued a formal order banning a proposed strike called by the All Japan Joint Struggle Committee of Labour Unions. US policy was increasingly dominated by its fear of communist influence in the unions. The American Federation of Labour sent one James Killen to act as SCAP's labour adviser and he organised a split in the trade union movement.[47] The imposition of the Dodge Line led to bankruptcies, closures and big cutbacks in the public sector. Japanese National Railways sacked nearly 100,000 workers and the Post Office and the Telegraph and Telephone Corporation got rid of another 220,000 between them.[48] These redundancies and others like them were used to purge militants, the more so because they coincided with the onset of the Cold War. In a speech on Constitution Day in 1950 General MacArthur suggested that SCAP would welcome the banning of the Communist Party.

The anti-communist witch hunt which followed in the Korean War was extremely deep. Thousands of leftists were driven out of workplaces. An anti-communist US source records:

By the end of [1950], at least 11,000 labour leftists had been fired from more than 20 industries; more than 1,000 lost jobs in governmental services and enterprises which had experienced the most militant labour activities, while similarly inclined unions in key private industries were also weakened. The process undoubtedly involved widespread disregard of basic civil and human rights.

    Not only communists but also other activists on the 'struggle committees' of unions were dismissed, and this usually involved the loss of their union membership. After the outbreak of the Korean War in June, 'security risks' were fired from companies with 'special procurement' contracts.[49]

Needless to say, the right wing Socialist Party was only too happy to collaborate with SCAP in getting control over the labour movement. Unions were split and company unions were set up. The Japanese working class was comprehensively defeated.[50]

It is important not to exaggerate the extent of the social peace established in the early Cold War period. It is true that in an atmosphere of intense anti-communism many of the gains that workers had won in the immediate post-war period were either lost again or transformed into their opposite. A good example of the latter process was the system of 'lifetime employment' and 'seniority wages'. Although these were based on older Japanese methods designed to retain skilled workers in periods of acute labour shortage, after the war they had been forced on the managements of the industrial companies by a combination of labour shortages and working class agitation. They were perceived by workers as a step towards establishing stable and secure careers for themselves.[51] After the collapse of the wave of militancy it was still in the interests of the employers to retain these concessions. The rapid expansion of the economy meant that there was an acute shortage of skilled labour and employers wanted to hold on to what they had got.[52]

At the same time, the hardening of the control of the bureaucracy of the unions, and sometimes the destruction of genuine unions and their replacement by purely company outfits, meant that this system now became much more of a device for disciplining workers and ensuring that they met productivity targets: the penalty for refusal was to be cast out of secure employment and to enter a world of erratic and badly paid work. The transformation of Japanese trade unionism was clearly illustrated by the aftermath of the Nissan strike of 1953. In the middle of a bitter dispute a new scab company union was set up. Among the slogans adopted at its founding meeting were:

—*Those who love the union love the company.*
—*A cheerful union, a cheerful life.*
—*A truly free and democratic union does not produce dictators.*
—*Avoid shifting the burden to workers in a thorough rationalisation of company operations.*
—*Fight for wages that promote the desire to work.*
—*Strengthen the management council and utilise capable individuals.*
—*Guarantee a wage based on productivity increases.*
—*Destroy the 'kept union' that is tied to the Japanese Communist Party.*[53]

In collaboration with this 'union', management were able to defeat the strike and sack the leaders of the real union.

Despite these serious defeats Japanese workers continued to press for concessions. The annual Spring Strike (the Shunto) is a ritualised procedure but it is still an expression of the fact that the Japanese working class retains a certain independence from the employers. However corrupt the union bureaucrats may be it is in their interests to demonstrate, both to their members and to the bosses, that they are not merely pawns of management.

Political opposition to Japanese capitalism remained strong. Right up to the present, workers vote for the Japanese Socialist and Communist Parties. Although the latter long ago abandoned revolutionary Marxism and became simply a left reformist party, it is much better supported than the equally craven British CP ever was. It has a strong group of MPs. Labour unions run independent candidates who win seats in both houses of parliament. The student movement of the 1960s was even more radical and bitter than its European and US counterparts, providing many of the militants who, together with local peasants, fought pitched battles with riot police against the plans to build a new airport at Narita, outside Tokyo. Opposition to nuclear weapons, war and imperialism has always been capable of mobilising the Japanese opposition on a large scale. There was widespread opposition to Japan taking sides in the Gulf War. Even today disgust at the behaviour of individual members of the US occupying forces provokes large scale demonstrations in which there is a strong anti-imperialist element. There is a strong strand of discontent and militancy which runs through Japanese politics from the earliest days up to the present.[54]

Nevertheless, the social peace established by a combination of political repression and rising living standards was real. It is important to remember that living standards of Japanese workers have been transformed in the course of the working life of a generation. The very success of Japanese capitalism enabled it to deflect the class conflict of the post-war period into the kinds of class collaboration which are the envy of their Western rivals. Opposition to Japanese capitalism was and is real, but it has been a minority current since the 1940s.

The evolution of Japanese capitalism has not yet produced the conditions that have destroyed this social peace. On the contrary, the recent recession and the slowing down of expansion have led to some symptoms of retreat. Union membership fell as a proportion of the total of employed workers after its peak in 1950. The 1960s saw an expansion both in the total number of union members and in their relative weight in the workforce, but the uncertainties after that slowed down the absolute growth and reversed the rise in union density. Between 1980 and 1990

the absolute number of union members fell very slightly, but the proportion of workers in unions fell from 30.8 percent to 25.2 percent.[55] The
ratio of workers belonging to labour unions hit a post-war low of 23.8
percent in 1995, falling 0.3 of a percentage point from the previous year.
An official of the labour ministry attributed the low figure to workforce
growth in the service sector where the level of unionisation is low. A
survey covering all of Japan's labour unions as of the end of June found
that membership had dropped for the first time in six years to total of
12,614,000, down 85,000 from the previous year, while employment
was up 300,000 to 53,090,000. At companies with 1,000 or more
employees 59.9 percent of workers belonged to labour unions, up 0.1
point, while the ratio dropped in smaller companies.[56]

The number of workers engaged in the Spring Offensive has continued to rise, but in recent years the size of the real wage increases they
have been able to win has fallen; 1995 also saw a number of unions, for
example the Telecom Workers' Union, announce before entering wage
negotiations that they would not be resorting to strike action whatever
the outcome.[57] Not surprisingly, the initial offer and final settlements
were smaller than the year before, repeating a trend which has become
well established in the 1990s.[58] Overall, however, management have
been able to ensure that wage rises have been paid for in productivity
increases.[59]

It is important to note that this is still a situation in which real wages
for employed workers are rising, albeit at a slower rate than in the past.
At the same time, unemployment was officially 2.2 percent in 1992 but
in reality was probably nearer 4 or 5 percent.[60] In November 1995 it had
reached a record 3.4 percent, the highest since 1953. This represented a
true figure of nearer 6 percent. Among young people the rate is much
higher, reflecting the standard Japanese strategy of reducing recruitment
in difficult periods rather than firing experienced workers. The official
rate of 6 percent may translate into 10 or 12 percent in reality. Although
all these figures are high by Japanese standards, they are still relatively
low by the standards of other developed capitalist countries. As we know
from the experience of Britain in the early 1980s, rising real wages combined with the fear of unemployment can lead to bitter isolated struggles
but make it very difficult to produce a generalised working class offensive.

It is not true that Japanese workers never go on strike, but they are
much less likely to do so than are their sisters and brothers in, for
example, Britain. As Table 1 shows, not only was the rate of strikes low
in the 1980s but it actually fell rather quickly during that decade.[61] If one
allows for the fact that the working class in Japan is much larger than
that in Britain, then the much lower level of strike activity in Japan is

even more evident. While the boom of the late 1980s did not follow a series of striking working class defeats in Japan, as it did in Britain, it was nevertheless true that there was a decline in the level of working class militancy.

TABLE 1: STRIKE DAYS IN JAPAN AND THE UK

DATE	JAPAN	UK
1980	1,001,000	10,964,000
1985	261,000	6,042,000
1989	220,000	4,028,000

Adding to these general problems is the fact that working class organisation is very patchy indeed. In companies with 1,000 workers or more, an average of 58.7 percent are members of unions. In companies in the mid-range, with 100-999 employees, it falls sharply to 23.3 percent. In small companies, with fewer than 100 workers, it is a mere 1.8 percent.[62] As we saw above, the gap is still widening. Of course, the figure for larger companies includes many workers who are in what are effectively company unions more interested in production targets than representing workers' interests, but the difference is still very sharp indeed. The problem is compounded by the continuation of the subcontracting system described above. The sharp difference between permanent workers in full time employment in large industries and the mass of workers in smaller industries and services has not disappeared as a result of this. In terms of wages, some estimates even suggest that the gap between rewards in large and small companies has got wider over the last decade.[63] The internal divisions inside the Japanese working class remain as great as they ever were.

Conclusions

Neither the rapid past growth of the Japanese economy nor its current slowing down are mysterious phenomena only to be explained by the unique properties of the Japanese themselves. On the contrary, the trajectory of Japanese capitalism involves four of the most general features of 20th century capitalism: a measure of state capitalism; combined and uneven development; the permanent arms economy; a divided and defeated working class. These elements have been present separately elsewhere in world capitalism. What was unique about Japan in the epoch of extremely rapid growth was the way in which they were combined together.

This combination gave Japanese capitalism a powerful competitive advantage, particularly as compared with US capitalism, which bore the direct cost of the permanent arms economy, had a state that was relatively reluctant to intervene in the detailed running of the economy, and was already a fully developed capitalist economy. On the back of those comparative advantages Japanese capitalism was able to develop modern industry, to transform the social structure of the country, and to build up a substantial export surplus.

Today Japanese capitalism is paying the price for its earlier successes. World expenditure on armaments has fallen dramatically just as Japan's own has begun to rise a little beyond the 1 percent limit. While there are still massive unevennesses in the labour market, there is no longer a ready supply of cheap labour that can be sucked in from the land in times of boom and expelled back to the family in the slump. The internationalisation of the economy has tended to make strong state action both less effective and less defensible internationally. The export success of Japanese capitalism has driven up the value of the yen relative to the dollar and forced business to try to find ways of increasing the rate of exploitation. At the same time, Japan has started to export capital and build manufacturing plants elsewhere. These in turn threaten the delicate social peace of Japan as industry is hollowed out in favour of lower cost economies and the threat of unemployment becomes ever more real.

This is the historic crisis which Japanese capitalism faces. It lies behind the headlines of endangered banks and reflationary packages. The current slump is deeper and longer than its predecessors precisely because the resources which enabled Japan to avoid the worst effects of the business cycle in the past no longer operate to the same extent. On top of that historic crisis, there are the consequences of the speculative boom in property prices that marked Japan in the late 1980s. The difficult business of liquidating the bad debts inherited from that period is as much of a problem for regenerating economic growth in Japan as it is in Britain.

It is this history that lies behind the political and social upheavals that occupy so much space in Western newspapers. Again, the doings of strange religious sects, government corruption and incompetence in the face of natural disasters, waves of social panic and continuous political crises are not uniquely Japanese phenomena. On the contrary, they are symptoms of the very real psychic price which must be paid for a successful and integrated capitalism economy. They are evidence of the human cost of the Japanese miracle every bit as much as murderously decaying cities, bomb planting militiamen and wild Christian extremists are evidence of the cost of the American Dream.

In neither case, of course, do these symptoms of social crisis amount to the same thing as class based opposition to the system. There is a long history of such opposition in Japan as much as in the US or anywhere else but, apart from great crises like the aftermath of military defeat, it has always been a minority current.

It is important, however, to be clear about the depth of the crisis facing Japanese capitalism today. There are signs of a modest recovery in the economy, but these come only after six years of deep recession which has persisted in the face of four massive government attempts to restart economic growth. There is every indication that this faltering recovery has come too late. The experience of the longest slump since the Second World War has marked a major change in Japanese life and its effects are felt at all levels.

At the political level the ruling class remains deeply divided. Despite the fact that the government is dominated by one wing of the old Liberal Democratic Party, deputies from another one of the splinters, the Shinshinto, together with deputies from the Communist Party, occupied the Budget Committee Room in the Diet for nearly a month in an effort to prevent the passage of the 1996 Finance Bill. They were responding to popular protests against the plan to bail out the heavily indebted jusen finance houses which are the main casualties of the collapse of property prices after the 1980s boom. On one estimate, the total debts of the jusen amount to $US100 per head for every man, woman and child in Japan.

This political unravelling echoes through all the parties and, similarly to the situation in Italy, is the root cause which has led to the exposure of the illegal activities of the former governing party. The trials and jailings reach right to the heart of the business and political elite. For example, in March 1996, Hiroyasu Watanabe, the former president of Tokyo Sagawa Kyubin Co, was jailed for seven years for his part in a 402,000,000 yen fraud. He had been engaged in illegal dealing with the leaders of the Inagawa-kai crime syndicate, at the behest of Shin Kanemaru, formerly vice-president of the LDP. He wanted the crime syndicate to call off a harassment campaign run by Nihon Kominto, an extreme right wing political grouping closely linked to them, against former prime minister Noboru Takeshita. In return for this political favour, the gangsters got huge illegal payouts.[64]

The economic effects of the crisis continue to be widely felt. Quite apart from the problems of the jusen, the rest of the banking sector is still in serious trouble.[65] The jusen themselves are closely linked to the main commercial banks, who continue to carry liability for their debts. The best that banks with huge portfolios of bad debts tied to land speculation can hope for is that the rate of fall in land prices will continue to slow down. Land prices have been falling continuously in the main industrial centres for the last five years. In 1995, in Tokyo itself, residential land prices fell 14 percent and commercial land prices fell 20.3 percent. The

Ginza district of Tokyo, a bit like Bond Street and Fifth Avenue rolled into one, remains the most expensive real estate in the world, but even there land prices fell more than 20 percent in 1995. Land there is worth roughly one third of what it could command in 1991. Residential land in Chiyoda-ku, the most expensive in Japan, has fallen from 12,300,000 yen per square metre in 1991 to a current value of 3,300,000 yen per square metre.[66] The owners (in this particular case former LDP prime minister Toshiki Kaifu), and the banks who funded their speculation, have problems of negative equity which make those in London look negligible. Faced with these problems, banks continue to merge and even to collapse. The closure of the Taiheiyo Bank at the end of March 1996 was the sixth within 12 months. It sent even larger shivers through the financial world because it was a listed bank closely tied to some of the largest of Japanese finance houses.

Of course, none of this spells the end of Japanese capitalism. The long years of accumulation have meant that some sectors of industry, particularly engineering and consumer electronics, are the most productive in the world. The state may no longer enjoy the same close relationship with big business, but it is still in a position to bail out financial institutions which find themselves in difficulties. Above all, Japanese capitalism continues to enjoy the benefits of a divided workforce in which many of the best rewarded sections are organised into tightly controlled company unions who see their main task as improving the competitive position of their firm.

These phenomena will not vanish overnight, although the competitive advantage is being visibly eroded on a daily basis. There is every sign that the Japanese ruling class is preparing to mount an attack on the working class as part of its recovery plan. Contrary to the trend in the 1990s, the 1996 Shunto resulted in a settlement higher than that for 1995. Toyota, the strongest of the car companies, offered 8,700 yen on monthly wages against a union demand for 9,000 yen, but refused to move towards a shorter working week by cutting 20 minutes from the daily hours. This will set the going rate throughout the motor industry, and there will be similar settlements in other major sectors.[67]

The tradition in Japan is that wage rises are set by sector rather than by company. This works reasonably well in periods of economic growth, but in recessions the weaker companies find themselves under pressure to make lower offers. As one commentator wrote:

> *Though the metals industries (including steel and autos) quadrupled their productivity between 1970 and 1992, the productivity of other industries only doubled during the same period... Despite the disparity in productivity, real hourly wages doubled in both the metals industry and the other industries. In*

fact, the rate of increase was slightly higher in the other industries. [68]

The public response to this year's settlement suggests that there will be attempts by the employers to break with the tradition of the Shunto. In the future, there will be attempts to settle wage disputes on a company basis, taking into account the trading position of each firm.

Another major target will be the 'life-time employment system'. As we have seen, this was always restricted to permanent employees of large companies, and did not include the mass of workers outside this privileged layer. However, even this is proving a burden in the recession. In particular, the fact that wage rates are tied to seniority rather than productivity is now seen as an increasing problem for companies facing increasing international competition. There have already been one or two well publicised attacks on this practice. For example, JAL, the flag carrying national airline, sacked all its permanent cabin staff and rehired them on temporary contracts. It is likely that these sorts of attacks will become more frequent in the future, and attempts will be made to tie wage levels more directly to productivity gains.

It is against this background that we have to consider the prospects for socialist ideas. The tiny handful of revolutionaries in Japan face an extremely difficult task. Socialists still face quite high levels of official repression in both workplace and society. Isolation and persecution together can produce political currents which veer sharply to the ultra-left. In the past this has been one of the problems facing the Japanese left, which has found itself isolated even from the quite large numbers of workers who are disillusioned with the system. Avoiding those traps while still providing a clear pole of attraction to militants looking for alternatives to the relentless grind of increasing productivity will be a very difficult task to undertake successfully.

There are some small signs that the deadening consensus of the past is starting to break up under the pressures of the long recession. Groups who in the past have been silent have begun to make their voices heard. In 1994, for the first time ever, there were Gay Pride demonstrations in Tokyo and Osaka. They were fairly small and not repeated in 1995, but they were a sign that the ideological prison is beginning to crumble. A similar example of the challenge to the central values of Japanese society were a number of small demonstrations by women. Unemployment amongst new female graduates is running at around 50 percent and women are being forced out of the workforce. The demonstrations, protesting against the high levels of sexual harassment at work and in job interviews, represented an unprecedented revolt against an entrenched subordinate status.

Even more significant, although very small in scale, has been a recent revolt against the class collaboration of Japanese unions. A group of workers in Shizwaka Prefecture, disgusted with the supine position of the official trade unions, have recently set up a new 'General Workers' Union'. It is tiny, and may yet face the fate of other breakaway unions unable to win large scale support. It is, however, very much a sign of the times. Some sections of the Japanese working class are starting to question the very basics of the system under which they have lived all their working lives and which, until recently, appeared to be unstoppably successful, but is now revealed as vulnerable. Those sorts of developments, although far from challenging the core of Japanese capitalism, constitute real and fresh opportunities for revolutionary ideas to begin to win an audience in the Japanese working class.

Notes

1   S Moffett, 'Press to Start', *Far Eastern Economic Review*, 21 December 1995, p16.
2   Y Kobayashi, 'Japan's 1996/1997 Draft Budget Aims to Spur Recovery', *Reuters News Service*, 20 December 1995.
3   H Sender, 'On the Chin', *Far Eastern Economic Review*, 8 June 1995, pp40-42.
4   H Macgregor, 'Japan to use controversial Cold War law to disband cult', *Los Angeles Times*, 15 December 1995.
5   R Skelton, 'Japan: The Battle on Japan's Streets', *Sydney Morning Herald*, 27 December 1995.
6   M Ishizuka, 'Japan: Nature's power—Man's terror struck amid economic, political chaos', *The Nikkei Weekly*, 25 December 1995.
7   *The Economist* is particularly prone to this. Tying itself in knots, it abandons its usual stress on hard money and calls for Keynesian measures to end the recession while at the same time giving regular dire warnings that the collapse of the Japanese banking system is almost upon us.
8   In *The Guardian*, 17 January 1995.
9   The most developed version of this thesis is the widespread body of writing and thought in Japan called 'nihonjinron'. In some versions, adherents of this school argue, for example, that there are differences in the functioning of Western and Japanese brains, and even that there are Western and Japanese types of honey bees (P N Dale, *The Myth of Japanese Uniqueness*, Routledge, 1990).
10 *The Economist, The Shape of the World Today* (Hutchinson, 1989), p234.
11 M Ito, *The World Economic Crisis and Japanese Capitalism* (Macmillan, 1990), p140.
12 Ibid, pp145-46.
13 Whether or not the Meiji restoration was a bourgeois revolution was an important political debate for the Japanese left in the 1920s, particularly for the Communist Party. In the prevailing, Stalinist, atmosphere it followed that if the Meiji restoration had been a bourgeois revolution, then the next 'stage' was a proletarian revolution. If, on the other hand, it had been something else, and Japan was still 'feudal', it followed that the next 'stage' would be a bourgeois revolution. If this was the case, it was logical to find a revolutionary bourgeoisie to ally with and to subordinate the interests of the working class to that end. See G Hoston, *Marxism and the Crisis of Development in Prewar Japan* (Princeton University Press, 1986). The same issue also became important for the US, although in rather a

different way. The occupation government (SCAP) started its reign with a commitment to democratising Japanese society. In this it was partly influenced by the leftist academic E H Norman, who argued that the Meiji restoration had been fundamentally authoritarian and undemocratic. The policy which followed from that was a radical break with the old order. Under the pressures of working class militancy, and later the Cold War, SCAP started to look for local allies. An alternative theory, most associated with E O Reischauer, stressed the democratic elements in the pre-war period, thus sanitising a section of the Japanese ruling class with whom it would be possible to collaborate. See J Dowers' introduction to the extremely interesting collection of essays by Norman in J Dower (ed), *Origins of the Modern Japanese State: Selected Writings of E H Norman* (Random House, 1975). For a summary of the main debates from a Marxist viewpoint, see Colin Barker's unpublished paper, 'Japan: Background and Significance of the Meiji Restoration of 1868'.

14   This argument about the nature of a revolution being determined by the historical problems that it carried out was best developed by T Cliff in a classic article which is regrettably long out of print. In it, he argued that the classic tasks of the bourgeois revolution, including national development, had in practice been carried out by a number of different social forces, particularly by the Stalinist parties that came to power in developing countries. It followed that one of the main functions of state capitalism was to carry out precisely the historical tasks undertaken by the bourgeoisie in earlier revolutions. Notably, the forced industrialisation so characteristic of state capitalist regimes had as its closest historical parallel the primitive accumulation of capital by the classic bourgeoisies in Britain and elsewhere. The parallel between the development of capitalism in Japan and the trajectory of state capitalism proper is a suggestive one which will recur at various points in this article. Although it is useful both to help understand the nature and dynamics of Japanese capitalism, it is important not to push the analogy too far. Japan is a quite different kind of historical formation than, say, China or North Korea. Japanese capital and the Japanese state are very heavily intertwined, but they are not identical.

15   S Vlastos, 'Opposition Movements in early Meiji, 1868-1885' in M Jensen (ed), *The Cambridge History of Japan: Volume 5, The Nineteenth Century* (Cambridge University Press, 1989), p382.

16   J Halliday, *A Political History of Japanese Capitalism* (Monthly Review Press, 1975).

17   Ibid, p82-96.

18   Ibid, pp116-140.

19   N Bukharin, *Imperialism and the World Economy* (Merlin Press, 1972). He wrote: 'A successful war requires that factories and plants, mines and agriculture, banks and stock exchanges — everything should "work" for the war... The exigencies of war, and of imperialist preparations for war, force the bourgeoisie to adopt a new form of capitalism, to place production and distribution under state power, to destroy completely the old bourgeois individualism' (p155).

20   To be convinced of that one only has to consider the most elementary figures. The key weapon in the Pacific war was the fleet aircraft carrier. Between Pearl Harbour and surrender, Japanese industry completed none of these complex and expensive ships. United States industry completed 32.

21   Still the best account of this, in our opinion, is that provided by M Kidron in *Western Capitalism Since the War* (Weidenfeld and Nicholson, 1968).

22   Kidron's elegant statement of the case runs thus: 'In so far as capital is taxed to sustain expenditure on arms it is deprived of resources that might otherwise go

towards further investment; in so far as expenditure on arms is expenditure on a fast wasting end product it constitutes a net addition to the market for "end" goods. Since one obvious result of such expenditure is high employment and, as a direct consequence of that, rates of growth amongst the highest ever, the dampening effect of such taxation is not readily apparent. But it is not absent. Were capital left alone to invest its entire pre-tax profit, the state creating demand as and when necessary, growth rates would be very much higher. Finally, since arms are a "luxury" in the sense that they are not used, either as instruments of production or as means of subsistence, in the production of other commodities, their production has no effect on profit rates overall' (Ibid, p39).

23   Ibid, p40.
24   T Uchino, *Japan's Postwar Economy* (Kodansha International, 1983), pp56-57. The 'Dodge Line' or 'Dodge Plan' was a policy of severe deflation imposed on the Japanese economy by US ambassador Joseph Dodge. Among his notes on his objectives was one of those phrases which ring with the irony of history: 'Get the country into hard condition for the struggle in the export market...'
25   C D Elston, 'The financing of Japanese industry', *Bank of England Quarterly Bulletin* (vol 21, no 4, December 1981), pp510-518.
26   W Eltis, 'The Lessons for the UK and for Europe from Asian Hyper-Growth', Gresham College lecture, London, 29 April 1994, chart 1.
27   M Cusumano, *The Japanese Automobile Industry* (Harvard University Press, 1985), pp241-261.
28   A Ernst, 'The Changing Nature and Persistence of Dualism in the Japanese Labour Market', *IFO Digest*, 3/92, p30.
29   M Ito, op cit, p151.
30   Ibid, p149.
31   Ibid, p182.
32   Figures for the 1960s and 1970s taken from *Fuji Bank Bulletin*, March-April 1988, p2. Figures for the 1980s taken from W Eltis, op cit, chart 1.
33   Y Sasajima, *Labor in Japan* (Foreign Press Centre, 1993), p19.
34   S Cockerill, 'The Japanese miracle explodes', *Socialist Review*, Issue 54, May 1983, p22.
35   J Woronoff, *Japan: the Coming Economic Crisis* (The Lotus Press, 1981), p240.
36   'Brittan Urges Cooperation With Japan: US trade approach said dated', *The Japan Times*, 22 March 1996, p7.
37   J Choy, *Japan Economic Institute Report* (Japan Economic Institute of America, October 6 1995). One dispute, for example, has the US government protesting that ships are not unloaded in Japanese ports on weekends. This scandalous interference with free trade arises from the fact that Japanese dockworkers had won a contract which gave them weekends off.
38   See C Kossis, 'A miracle without end? Japanese capitalism and the world system', *International Socialism*, 2:54, pp106-110.
39   E Graham and N Anzai, 'The myth of a de facto Asian economic bloc: Japan's foreign direct investment in East Asia', *Columbia Journal of World Business*, Fall 1994, vol 29, number 3, pp16-21.
40   H Sender, 'Nippon's Choice', *Far Eastern Economic Review*, 8 June 1995, pp38-40.
41   M Cusumano, op cit, pp267ff.
42   J Crump, *The Origins of Socialist Thought in Japan* (Croom Helm, 1983).
43   S Garon, *The State and Labor in Modern Japan* (University of California Press, 1987), pp39ff.
44   Ibid, p225.

45 M Farley, 'Labor Policy in Occupied Japan', excerpted in J Livingston, J Moore and F Oldfather (eds), *Postwar Japan: 1945 to the Present* (Random House, 1973), p141.
46 J Moore, *Japanese Workers and the Struggle for Power: 1945-47* (University of Wisconsin Press, 1983). This is a book well worth reading.
47 H Bix, 'American Labor and Japanese Unionists', Livingston et al (eds), op cit, pp172-173.
48 T Uchino, op cit, p52.
49 A Cole, G Totten, and C Uyehara, 'Labor and the Red Purge', Livingston et al (eds), op cit, p175.
50 J Halliday, op cit, pp217-220.
51 A Gordon, *The Evolution of Labor Relations in Japan* (Harvard University Press, 1985), pp 339-366.
52 Ibid, pp367-411.
53 M Cusumano, op cit, p156.
54 See R Mouer and Y Sugimoto, *Images of Japanese Society* (KPI, 1986), pp106-115.
55 Y Sasajima, op cit, p56.
56 *JIJI Newswire*, 26 December 1995.
57 H Kato, 'Unions take no-strike vow before wages talks', *Nikkei Weekly*, 25 February 1995.
58 F Sumio, 'Record low wage hikes expected in key industries', *Nikkei Weekly*, March 27 1995.
59 M Greiner, C Kask, C Sparks, 'Comparative manufacturing productivity and unit labor costs', *Monthly Labor Review*, February 1995, vol 118, number 2, pp26-39. [C Sparks is no relation to one of the current authors].
60 Y Sasajima, op cit, p16.
61 Figures from a private communication from Mark Baxendale.
62 Y Sasajima, op cit, p56.
63 Y Sasajima, op cit, p47.
64 'Ex-Tokyo Sagawa chief gets seven years in prison', *The Japan Times*, 23 March 1996, p1.
65 G Barker, 'Humbling of the giants' in '*Financial Times* Survey: Japanese Financial Markets', *The Financial Times*, 28 March 1996, pIII.
66 'Commercial Plots Plummet: Land prices in main urban areas fall for fifth year', *The Japan Times*, 22 March 1996, p2.
67 'Wage talks reach climax as key sectors offer raises', *The Japan Times*, 22 March 1996, p1.
68 T Tsuyoshi, 'It's time to change the shunto system', *The Nikkei Weekly*, 11 March 1996, p7.

When science fails us

RICHARD LEVINS

The following article is an address given by Richard Levins on his receipt of the 1996 Edinburgh Medal during the 1996 Edinburgh International Science Festival.[1]

Modern European and North American science has developed technologies which promised a deeper understanding of the world and a better life for humanity. And indeed, its achievements are impressive: we can read the composition of distant galaxies from tired bits of ancient light, we can decipher the histories of the rocks formed a billion years ago and the diets of species long gone. We can track the movements of molecules and of caribou, sequences of genes and civilisations. We have bred plants and animals to fit our technologies, invented new ways of communicating and of diagnosing diseases and of predicting the weather.

But science also has had dramatic failures. The promises of understanding and progress have not been kept, and the application of science to human affairs has often done great harm. Public health institutions were caught by surprise by the resurgence of old diseases and the appearance of new ones. Modern planning has not given us more habitable cities. Industrial design for greater efficiency has not made work more humane but, instead, led to increased bodily stress, anxiety, overwork and unemployment. Pesticides increase pests, create new pest problems and contribute to the load of poison in our habitat. Antibiotics create new pathogens resistant to our drugs. Modern high-tech agronomy watches our soils disappearing. The green revolution did not eliminate hunger but increased the polarisation between rich and poor and the dependence of developing countries on imports. Scientific theories have even been put forth to justify inequality, racism, aggression and competitiveness.

I am sure that all of you could add to the list of major problems that science has not only not solved but has even made worse through the impact of technologies that intervene strongly into complex processes with simple-minded expectations. It is no wonder that we see an anti-science backlash involving not only cuts in expenditures for research and the education of scientists, but also the turning of young people away from the scientific vocations, a counterposing of scientific knowledge to humane or spiritual feelings and morality, and attacks on scientific rationality itself.

It is, therefore, natural that scientists and other intellectuals rush to the defence of science. But some of the criticisms which have been made are valid. There are two very different kinds of criticism, one conservative and one radical, coming from very different sources and pursuing very different goals. On the one hand, conservative criticism rejects the very idea that science should aim to understand the world in order to guide our actions. Its advocates often brush aside scientific evidence in favour of theological claims. They misuse the mathematics of 'chaos' to deny the essential intelligibility of the world. They recognise the social conditioning and the ultimate fallibility of science but use it as an excuse for refusing to distinguish the relatively true from the dreadfully wrong. These critics usually praise technology while damning the intellectual independence of science that made that technology possible. Their ideal would be technically well trained, docile and specialised researchers inventing ever newer and more sophisticated means while remaining unreflective about ends.

Radical criticism shares the old scientific goal of understanding the world for making life better. It taxes science for its failure to live up to its own stated principles. Military secrecy and corporate proprietary rights directly deny access to knowledge. The high cost of research denies such access in practice. We can no longer undertake the independent verification that was the cornerstone of the democracy of science and the guarantor of its objectivity. The costs of education and general economic inequalities make access to the scientific community a matter of privilege. Hierarchies of credibility and vocabularies for putting down uncomfortable ideas, such as 'far out', 'faddish', 'cranky', 'not mainstream', 'ideological' or 'unproven', negate the spirit of open minded inquiry. The need for continued funding and prestige make it important to be first and to be right rather than to be self-critical and open. A cult of expertise and established credentials thwarts the democratic, egalitarian spirit of science which means that arguments are in fact not given equal opportunity regardless of their source.

This radical criticism also challenges some of the core principles of science. The demand to examine ideas without reference to their source, which is an expression of elementary fairness, can also prevent us from understanding the context of innovation, and therefore the reasons for science following one agenda and not another. The call to separate thinking from feeling or facts from wishes, so crucial in the struggle for objectivity, can also encourage the passive impersonal mode of scientific writing that hides the history of, and reasons for, an investigation. It has allowed scientists to participate in the most heinous crimes with a sense of righteousness.

A good radical criticism aims at a democratic, humane and creative science that looks at our relations with the rest of nature in its broadest context, and would combine specialised research with self-reflection and with frequent re-examination of goals. It would seek a renovation of science reviving some of the old traditional goals but also propose new ones.

In what follows I will discuss three areas where scientific disciplines have had great success in the small but failed us in the large. I will then consider some of the common features in their failure and finally suggest a programme for the revitalisation of science.

The epidemiological transition

Two or three decades ago the expectation was that infectious disease would decline and be replaced by chronic disease as the major health problem in the world. This expectation was labelled the epidemiological transition. It remained the prevailing dogma in public health even after the resurgence of malaria, tuberculosis, cholera and dengue, and the appearance of AIDS, Lyme disease, Ebola virus, Marburg virus, Lassa fever, toxic shock syndrome and Legionnaires' disease.

As each new disease appeared it was studied urgently and knowledge of the infective agent, how it was transmitted and possible approaches to treatment, appeared quickly. Genes were sequenced, tests invented and surveillance systems designed to detect new cases rapidly. But, despite all this, new diseases continue to appear and old ones continue to reinvade.

That science was caught by surprise by the resurgence of infectious disease is in itself not surprising. Surprise in science is inevitable because we have to study the new by treating it just like the old. The new *is* like the old. This makes science possible. But it is also unlike the old. This makes science necessary and simple experience insufficient. But it also makes surprise inevitable and guarantees that we eventually meet situations where our old ideas no longer hold good and perhaps never did.

However, we do have the obligation to understand why enormous errors were made and to recognise and correct them as soon as possible. In order to do this, we first have to understand why the idea that infection would decline seemed so plausible in the 1970s. My working hypothesis is that our scientific predecessors were just as smart as we are, and if they reached wrong conclusions they did so for good reasons.

There were three main arguments supporting the belief that infectious diseases would decline:

1) Infectious disease had been declining for over a century. Smallpox was on the verge of complete eradication. Tuberculosis was in retreat. A polio vaccine removed the annual panic of infantile paralysis.

2) New drugs, antibiotics, better vaccines, more subtle diagnostic techniques were being invented to increase our tool kit while our adversaries, the bacteria and viruses and fungi, had to rely on the same old tools of mutation and recombination. It seemed likely that this would tip the balance in our favour.

3) International economic development programmes to end poverty were proclaimed, and the new affluence would allow all countries the resources to apply the most modern techniques of disease control. It would also give us longer lives and an older population. Since most infectious diseases attack children, populations as a whole would be less vulnerable to them.

These were plausible arguments, but they were wrong. And the ways in which they were wrong prove very enlightening. A century or two is too short a time period to justify the claim of a definitive end to infectious disease. If we look instead at the longer sweep of human history we see diseases rise and fall. The first pandemic of plague that we can confirm in Europe emerged and subsided during the collapse of the Roman Empire, the second as feudalism entered its crisis in the 14th century. The conquest of the Americas was perhaps the most devastating epidemiological event of recorded history. Plague, smallpox, tuberculosis and other diseases combined with the hunger caused by the breakup of indigenous productive systems and direct massacres to reduce the population by as much as 90 percent in the two centuries following the arrival of Columbus. This public health disaster lasted two centuries and in some ways is not completely over today.

Thus the doctrine of the epidemiological transition is better replaced by the proposition: whenever there are large scale changes in society, climate, land use or population movements, there will also be new epidemiological problems. It was not a lack of knowledge of the past that caused this lack of attention to the long sweep of history. It was rather a sense that our own time represented so radical a break with the past that what happened back then was irrelevant or, in the famous phrase of Henry Ford, "History is bunk!"

There were other aspects to this narrowness of thinking about disease. Medical science is concerned only with one species, the human. But if public health workers had looked also at veterinary and plant disease then it would have been more obvious that disease is a general phenomenon of evolutionary ecology. All groups of animals and plants have parasites. There are even bacteria that parasitise protozoa, others that infect roundworms, and even bacteria and viruses that parasitise bacteria.

Parasitism involves complex patterns of adaptation and counteradaptation and there is no evidence for a long term trend to their elimination. Looking beyond the human species, scientists would have seen diseases spreading and contracting, spilling over into new hosts and presenting different symptoms, microbes competing with or enhancing each other's capacity for mischief. They would have been sensitive to the epidemiological consequences of deforestation, irrigation, new patterns of human settlement. The experience of agriculture shows that pests become resistant to pesticides and this would have reinforced the observations of drug and antibiotic resistance to warn that, whenever we change the conditions of survival for an organism, the evolutionary pressures on it will be changed and it will respond one way or another.

Disease is not merely a question of a pathogen finding a host, nor is medicine a question of a drug killing the pathogen. Whether a germ successfully establishes itself in a person, and whether it is able to invade a population, depends on the vulnerabilities of both. This is influenced by the status of the individual's immune system, which may be depressed by other diseases, malnutrition, stress, drugs and pollutants, and by other less well studied aspects of disease resistance.

Another aspect of the narrowness of thinking about disease is the separation of the biological from the social. A social epidemiology would begin with the proposition that human biology is a socialised biology. This is true of our physiology; eating, for example, is not understandable merely as the biochemistry of nutrition. What we eat or refuse to eat, who eats and who does not eat, how much we eat, who determines what is eaten, who you eat with or wouldn't be caught dead eating with, who prepares the food and who washes up, are all consequences not only of the physiological fact that we have to eat, but also the social arrangements around eating. Similarly, breathing is not a passive result of respiratory metabolism. How we breathe is related to stress, air quality, perceptions about the social environment and our emotions. Posture and biomechanical stress, the backaches and stiff necks and painful joints and muscles we experience, are not the passive consequence of our species walking erect but of who we are in society, what kind of work we do and what feelings we are expressing or suppressing, and what we are trying to convey with our postures. Pantomime actors grasp this exquisitely and in an instant convey to their audiences whether they own an estate or are slaves on that estate, whether they are important, dangerous, accommodating or insignificant. More obviously, sex cannot be understood simply as reproduction.

Human genetics and ecology are also social. If epidemiologists had been more sensitive to how society penetrates our bodies, genes would not be so readily accepted as providing sufficient explanations of the patterns of prevalence of diseases. All genes do is make proteins or influence when the proteins are made. What happens next depends on the environments within the cell, in the body as a whole, and in the community where that body develops. The process also depends on complex interactions among genes, the organism as a whole and the environment. Genes may influence the environments to which an organism is exposed. These environments then affect the rate of mutation of the genes. They determine which genetic differences show up as organism differences, and which genes are selected.

We have transformed our environments. The composition of our outdoor and indoor atmosphere has been supplemented by tens of thousands of new chemical compounds which interact in unsuspected ways. Productive activity takes place at temperatures, at paces, and at hours of the day and night that are historically new for our thermoregulatory mechanisms, our serotonin rhythms and our muscles. Giant cities and the special habitats of prisons, nursing homes, schools and refugee camps offer previously unexperienced population densities. Sealed buildings and barely recycled air in aeroplanes create new habitats for pathogens and increase exposures to airborne viruses. New patterns of alienation, social harassment and anxiety demand that our physiological and psychological responses which evolved to deal with emergencies now cope with chronic conditions. If we could step back from the details and squint we would see patterns; our societies make us sicker in a thousand ways and then invest ever more resources trying to repair the damage.

A social epidemiology could be sensitive to the complexity of the pathways linking general aspects of society through our nervous systems and neurotransmitters to the various kinds of white blood cells that fight infection and sometimes turn against us. The outcomes of infection depend on these same factors and also on the availability and effectiveness of medical care. They obviously are not distributed evenly across countries or within countries. They are certainly not distributed evenly across diseases, where the pattern of knowledge and ignorance is influenced by whose diseases they are.

The expectation that the new technologies of drugs, antibiotics, pesticides and vaccines would 'win the war' with the pathogens grossly underestimated both the dynamic capacity of organisms to adapt and the intricacies of natural selection. Microbes not only undergo mutation but can also receive genes from other species. Therefore, genetic variation is available for selection. Therapies that threaten the survival of the germs also focus natural selection on overcoming or evading those therapies. The genetic makeup of pathogen populations therefore shifts readily, not only in the long run but even in the course of a single outbreak and within a single host during a bout of illness. There are strong opposing demands on the pathogen's biology to select for access to nutrients, to avoid the body's defenses and exit to a new host. Variations in a body's state of nutrition, its immune system, the presence or absence of other infections, access to treatment, the treatment regime and conditions of transmission all push and pull the genetic makeup of pathogen populations in different directions. This means that we constantly see new strains arising, new strains that differ in their drug and antibiotic resistance, clinical course, virulence, and biochemical detail. Some even develop resistance to treatments that have not yet been used if these threaten the survival of the pathogens in ways similar to old treatments. As long as we see nature as passively absorbing the impacts of our interventions we will be caught by surprise by the failures of previously successful interventions.

Another reason why public health professionals expected the decline of infectious disease was the belief that the economic penetration of capitalism to the furthest reaches of the globe would eliminate hunger and provide healthcare for all people in all classes in all countries. This assertion was accepted implicitly without examination. It was part of the Cold War mythology and therefore challenges to it could be dismissed as enemy propaganda. Only now can mainstream social science acknowledge the growing gap both between rich and poor countries and within countries and ask why the earlier high expectations have not been realised. And only now can public health confront the growing inequalities as a serious public health issue.

Thus public health was caught by surprise because of several kinds of narrowness: a short time frame, limitation to only our own species, isolation from evolutionary ecology, and a failure to come to grips with the pressing social issues that affect vulnerability to disease. In order to be up to the task it faces, an integrated epidemiology would have long time horizons, broad species ranges, be rooted in evolutionary ecology and social theory. It would have to respect and study explicitly the structure and dynamics of complex systems and would look critically at its own history.

These are characteristics of what would be a dialectical epidemiology.

Of green revolutions

The problems and failures that beset public health have much in common with those in agriculture because agriculture is like medicine in many ways. The objects of interest in both fields are simultaneously biological and social. Researchers in both agriculture and health are trying to solve urgent problems of human welfare and therefore are often impatient of theory. Both have received generous public support as well as private corporate investment. The products of that massive research effort have frequently been turned into commodities and marketed for private gain.

In both medicine and agriculture practice often does more harm than good, often enough for us to have special terms to describe these failures: iatrogenesis, the causing of disease by doctors; nosocomial infections that arise in hospitals; secondary pests that become threats to food production only after intensive pesticide use. In both medicine and agriculture we have achieved great sophistication in the small, but this has been accompanied by a growing irrationality in the large. Finally, dissatisfaction with both fields has led to the growth of 'alternative' movements such as herbal medicine, homeopathy, naturopathy, organic and biodynamic farming.

Over the last few centuries average agricultural yields increased as a result of mechanisation, the use of chemicalisation (including fertilisers and pesticides), plant and animal breeding, and scientific management. Although problems arose, it was widely believed that such problems were the price of progress and would be solved by the same means that created them. But, starting in the 1960s, there has been increasing criticism of the high-tech pathway of agricultural development. The different criticisms have come from different sources and focus on different concerns, but they also flow together into a coherent theoretical and political critique:

1) Modern high-tech agriculture has not eliminated hunger.
2) It undermines its own productive base through erosion, soil compaction and salinisation, depletion of water resources and depletion of genotypic diversity.
3) It changes land use patterns, encouraging deforestation, draining of wetlands and planting crops according to market criteria even in unsuitable climates. It promotes a loss of crop diversity by specialisation and commercial seed production and reduces overall biodiversity through its chemical inputs and extensive monocultures.
4) It increases vulnerability to nature, especially to climate and microclimate change, pest outbreaks and atmospheric and water pollutants.

This is because of large scale monoculture, the selection of varieties for maximum yield under optimal conditions and the loss of beneficial fauna and flora.

5) It makes farming increasingly dependent on inputs from off the farm. This means that cash flow becomes increasingly important as fertilisers replace natural nitrogen fixers, irrigation replaces the broken hydrological flows and storages of water, and also because pesticides replace natural enemies of pests and hybrid seeds must be bought. Dependence on external inputs increases the vulnerability to price instability and politically motivated trade policies.

6) It debases food quality as regional specialisation increases storage and transport time and crops and techniques are chosen for quantitative yield. Specialisation makes even farmers dependent on buying food.

7) It increases the gap between rich and poor. The rich are able to buy, or get credit to buy, the new inputs, establish the marketing connections and average their returns across years. The poor, however, need to be successful every year. Modern agriculture especially undermines the economic independence of women. The new technologies are usually given to men, even in places where women traditionally did most of the farming. The new technologies make the domestic chores of women, such as gathering firewood and fetching water, more time consuming. Women's diverse activities in the home conflict with the extreme seasonality of commercial monoculture.

8) It poisons people, first the farm workers who handle pesticides, then their family members who handle the pesticide soaked clothing and drink water where pesticides and fertilisers have run into ground water. Finally it reaches those who eat the crops produced with pesticides and animals raised with antibiotics and growth hormones.

9) It also poisons other species, and the environment as a whole, with eutrophication of our waterways from fertiliser runoff, accumulation of pesticides in the body tissues of fish and birds, and nitrification of the air.

Despite its technical complexity, modern agricultural technology has a narrow intellectual base susceptible to surprise. The final conclusion, therefore, is that the commercialised, export oriented, high-tech agriculture is a non-sustainable successional stage in the ecology of production, like the shrubs that squeeze out the grasses and herbs of an abandoned field only to create the conditions for their own replacement by trees.

What I have described as a successional stage is seen by proponents of modernisation as a desirable end goal. Modernisation theory assumes that there is only a single pathway of development, along the single axis which runs from less developed to more developed. This leads to a further assumption; that the task of the less developed is to become like the more developed as quickly as possible.

Modernisation theory proposes that:
1) Progress moves from labour intensive to capital intensive production.
2) Progress moves from heterogeneous land use to homogeneous land use devoted to the most advantageous crop.
3) Progress moves from small scale to large scale to take advantage of large economies.
4) Progress moves from dependence on nature to control over or replacement of nature.
5) Progress requires the replacement of traditional knowledge, labelled 'superstition', by scientific knowledge.
6) In science, modernisation theory asserts that progress moves from broad general knowledge to increasingly narrow specialisation.
7) Progress moves from the study of natural objects to their smallest parts.

But an integrated, dialectical, agricultural science equally rooted in natural science and a critique of society would recognise that we have to move beyond the capital intensive model where great masses of energy are applied to move great quantities of matter. Instead, integrated agricultural science could point to a low input, gentle, thought intensive technology that nudges more than it commands and reduces dependence on purchased equipment and chemicals. Such a system would be less energy costly, preserving productive capacity, and protecting the human population and our habitats.

An integrated agricultural science would reject both the random heterogeneity of land use imposed by land tenure and the homogeneity of the plantation. It would propose a planned heterogeneity in a mosaic of land uses where each plot of land contributes harvestable products and also facilitates the production on the other plots. Forests would provide wood and fruit and honey but also modulate the flow of water, alter the microclimate out from the edge, house birds and bats that consume pests and, of course, offer restful shelter to people.

Pastures could provide not only livestock, but also manure for biogas and the fertilisation of vegetable beds, nectar sources for parasitic wasps that control pests. Pasture land could also fix nitrogen and control erosion. Elements of such a system are already in practice in many places. In Cuba alternating strips of bananas and sweet potatoes or intercrops of corn with sweet potatoes provide the shade and nesting sites that allow predatory ants to control pests of sweet potato. Occasional rows of corn among the peppers divert the fruitworms and so protect the peppers. Organic farmers in the US use marigolds to repel nematodes and beans to protect tomatoes from the late blight as well as to fix nitrogen. Maize roots reach deep down and bring up minerals from lower layers while shallow rooted crops hold the soil. Ponds produce fish and predatory dragonflies, ameliorate the microclimate, are a reservoir of water for fire fighting and a place to swim.

The unit of planning need not coincide with the unit of production. The size of plots needs to reflect the scales over which beneficial interactions occur. The mosaic of different land uses combines considerations of crop rotation with buffers against natural and economic uncertainty, a diverse diet and differential labour requirements. This would also lead to the compensating diversity of more and less profitable crops.

Modernisation's attempt to remove our subjection to the uncertainties of nature by a complete control over all the processes on a farm cannot be successful. But we can confront uncertainty through a mixed strategy of detection of problems in time to do something about them, prediction of likely events, design of a buffered system tolerant to a broad range of conditions, and by prevention. All of this requires intellectual detours from what is narrowly practical to understand the long and short term processes in all their complexity.

An integrated agroecology would respect both traditional and scientific knowledge. The one is derived from a detailed, intimate, perceptive and very specific familiarity that people have with their own circumstances. The other requires some distance from the particular in order to compare and generalise. Each has its areas of insight and its blindnesses, so that the best conditions for producing knowledge are those that allow farmers and scientists to meet as equals.

Agriculture has to be guided by a broader scientific vision. We must reject the reductionism that gives priority to molecules over cells and cells over organisms and organisms over populations. I insist that in addition to modern molecular biology there is also a modern physiology, modern anatomy, modern ecology, modern biogeography, modern sociology.

Protecting the environment

Environmental awareness is not new. Movements for the preservation of nature, usually of the relatively unexploited parts of nature, have existed for over a century. Concern for the inhabited environment also has a long history. In the US the Environment Protection Agency was established in 1970, and there are now many international agencies concerned with one or another aspect of environmental protection. As long ago as the 1920s, the Soviet Union had some of the earliest and most stringent and thoughtful (and unenforced) laws for environmental protection. Costa Rica has adopted a bold programme to set aside vast areas as national parks. Nevertheless, industry continues to pour CO_2 into the atmosphere, the forests still blacken under acid rain or yield to the chainsaw, fish populations decline and carcinogens accumulate. Ironically Costa Rica is leading the world in the rate of loss of rainforest to banana plantations and the impoverishment of peasants.

There have also been dramatic reversals of the destructive trends. There are salmon in the Thames again, and reforestation in Japan. The Hudson River is cleaner and smog has declined in London. It seems as if no local environmental problem, except for some of the radioactive contamination sites, is completely unremediable. However, each time a forest or pond is saved it becomes harder to save the next one. Arguments based on the idea of not 'going too far' are offered and supported by others which play off the environment against 'the economy'. Corporations that have never cared a fig about their workers suddenly become champions of job protection in order to have a free hand to cut down forests.

The history of environmental degradation is a history of greed, poverty and ignorance. By greed I do not mean the individual idiosyncratic greed that might yearn for three yachts where two would do. Rather I refer to the institutionalised greed of business that has to expand to survive, that is always looking for new products, ways to create new needs, ways to cut costs by reducing environmental safeguards or evading the enforcement of existing ones.

At a time when there is growing awareness of the need for an 'ecological society', the incompatibility of that goal with an economy driven by greed has not yet been assimilated. Proposals are still being offered to reconcile two very different modes of relating to nature.

While ecological necessity seeks sustainability, the commodified economy needs growth. This growth can be achieved by producing more of the same things, or by making familiar commodities bigger, more complicated or with more elaborate packaging. Growth can also be achieved by inventing new ways of turning natural conditions into resources for exploitation, by finding technical means for making more and more of our lives marketable, and by investing great effort into creating new needs for consumption. Although economists emphasise that needs lead to production, the other branch of the feedback loop increasingly represents reality; production leads to new needs as producers seek to create markets.

While ecology stresses interaction, environmental protection law depends on assessing separable liabilities. The courts cannot disentangle the complexities of nature so that sometimes awareness of interaction protects the polluters more than the environment.

Ecology values the uniqueness of materials, places and living things, but the economy sees them all as interchangeable commodities measured on the single scale of economic values. Therefore there is no special virtue in preserving a resource, only in making profit. It may be economically rational to use up a resource totally and then move to the next investment. While ecology values diversity, economic rationality favours going for the single most profitable crop, and great quantities of a single commodity, to benefit from economies of scale.

There do exist movements which are resisting untrammelled greed. The destruction of particular habitats has been detained, some noxious substances have been removed from the atmosphere, important victories have been won. But growth itself cannot be retarded, the valuing of nature on the single scale of money cannot be eliminated, and new hazards can be invented faster than they can be studied and outlawed. Thus the complexities and anomalies of protecting our environment arise from a deep conflict between the ecology and the economy.

Poverty is the poverty of communities that have to choose between starvation and suffocation, and often get both. The industries that come with promises of jobs are also committed to profitability through 'downsizing' the labour force, contracting out to non-union shops, increasing the working day and nibbling away at health and retirement and other benefits. They can then relocate to wherever costs are lowest. The governments of poor countries are convinced or coerced into allowing toxic dumping on their land, the plundering of their soils and sacrificing their forests to 'development'.

Poverty allows environmental degradation as a lesser evil when there is the urgent need to have food or money for food. It shortens the time horizon to the immediate urgencies. It forces people to use up their capacity to produce—forests, water reserves, soil quality, rare species—even when they know the new problems they are creating. It encourages Third World governments, and local governments of poor communities in rich countries, to tolerate violations of ecological standards and even to invite the dumping of toxic materials on their land in order to gain income. Poverty is usually accompanied by a lack of control by the poor over what will happen to them. Therefore longer term planning is neither a practical option nor a theoretical commitment. It is not reinforced by experience and, therefore, seems unreal as well as less urgent.

Ignorance is not the passive absence of information but a constructed mix of data, gaps in data, data about irrelevant things, unrealistic expectations, fragmented knowledge, rigid categories and false dichotomies. Ignorance hides the impact of economic activities and technical choices and it narrows the scope of inquiry. Ignorance also obscures the processes of choosing among alternatives by the use of euphemisms such as 'the economy' instead of profit, 'decision makers' instead of the owners or their representatives. It hides within the language of cost/benefit analysis the separation between those who pay the costs and those who get the benefits. It pretends that a neutral optimisation process reconciles the interests of all parties when more usually all it can do is ratify existing relations of power.

Greed, poverty and ignorance are not independent factors. Greed creates and maintains poverty and promotes ignorance. Poverty accedes to greed and creates the sense of urgency that dismisses long term vision as 'unrealistic' and complex analysis as 'just theoretical'. This in turn preserves ignorance in the name of practicality and that dismisses science as the luxury of the affluent countries that may be received by the poor countries, but not created by them. Ignorance justifies greed ِِِِِِِِِِِِِِِ natural and inevitable while rejecting all criticism of greed, thus guaranteeing poverty.

The general critique

The problems of health, agriculture and environment are complex problems. But so is engineering. Before the spaceship *Challenger* exploded it was quite common to hear the exasperated query, 'But how come we can put a man on the moon and yet not...?' The 'yet not' could be eliminate hunger or cure AIDS or save the rainforest or any other of a growing list of stubborn problems. The question was usually rhetorical, not a search for an answer but a cry of protest against misplaced priorities. But it is a serious question and deserves careful attention. I think there are three major reasons for the intractability of these problems.

First, there is the acceptance of hidden and unacknowledged side conditions. We want to provide healthcare for all, but subject to the side condition that the pharmaceutical industry continues to be private and profitable. Another condition, in backward countries such as mine, is that health insurance and even medical services are provided for gain. We want to preserve rural life, subject to the condition of not infringing on the power of the landed oligarchies. We want to respect the cultures and land rights of indigenous peoples, subject to the side condition that the oil monopolies can use the subsoil unimpeded. We want to encourage food production, subject to the side conditions that imported food products can enter the Third World markets freely and compete with peasant cultivators. We want a poison-free atmosphere, provided we do not intrude on the trade secrets of the polluters.

The second set of reasons are institutional. Ministries of health do not usually speak to ministries of agriculture and doctors do not talk to veterinarians or plant pathologists. This is especially a problem in the US where plant pathology and veterinary medicine are taught in the universities of the land grant system run by state governments while medical schools are usually in private urban universities. Corporations guard their product information from each other and the public. The systems of rewards and promotions for scientists place a premium on short term reductionist research that is most readily turned into marketable commodities.

The organisation of a research centre or university reflects and reinforces barriers among disciplines. Further, the studies of different objects are often arrayed on a hierarchical scale with ranking by the size of the object (the smaller ones being more 'fundamental') or along a 'hardness-softness' axis. In biology, the students of the small have appropriated the term 'modern' for their own fields.

Finally we come to the intellectual barriers to solving these problems. The problems are complex in ways different from engineering problems. In engineering the parts are produced outside of the wholes and perform in the laboratory more or less the way they will perform in the assembled systems. In eco-social systems it is not always clear what the appropriate 'parts' are, since they evolve and develop together and have only temporary existence away from their 'wholes'. The objects that have to be analysed together, for example the microbes themselves, the nutritional levels of populations and the behaviour of health bureaucrats, have all been assigned to different disciplines.

The barriers all derive from the very powerful reductionist strategy that created European and North American science in the first place and made possible both its dramatic successes and its special blindnesses. This strategy involved the choice of the smallest possible object as the 'problem', and the division of a problem into its smallest parts for analysis. Reductionism also meant the holding constant of everything but one factor at a time, the examination of static descriptions before looking at the dynamics and the subdivision of the research process itself into the separate stages of assembling the 'facts' and the making of theories. All these had their historical justifications in the struggle for scientific objectivity against several adversaries. These enemies included not only theological authoritarianism but also the introspections of natural philosophy and other unanchored speculations. The reductionist tactics have temporary value as moments in the scientific process. There is nothing wrong with identifying cell types or sequencing DNA or measuring energy. Then they are research tactics, and may be useful or not according to the specific situation. But as a philosophy of nature and society and as the dominant mode of investigation, reductionist tactics are responsible for many of the dramatic failures of scientific programmes.

It is necessary in all research to make distinctions, to identify objects of interest as separate from other objects, to recognise different kinds of processes and causes. But science often stops there, without then putting back together what it has separated physically or conceptually. It imagines that our own creations, what we do for purposes of study, are valid descriptions of reality. False dichotomies, such as heredity/environment, physical/psychological, equilibrium/change, science/ideology, thinking/feeling, biological/social, random/determined, order/chaos, lawfulness/historical contingency, lifestyle/social conditions, have wrought havoc with scientific analysis, because they force choices between alternatives that really are not mutually exclusive. Instead of confronting the richness of interaction and interpenetration, scientific analysis often resorts to statistical devices to assign relative weights to different factors. Once we have done this, we can imagine that we have described complexity when what we have really done is reduce that complexity to a sum of 'factors'. Criticism of these and other false dichotomies is a necessary step in the revitalisation of a science, making it capable of confronting the enormous problems our species is now facing, and such criticism is also a major aspect of a dialectical approach.

But when we abandon the reductionist programme, we are confronted with phenomena of daunting complexity, and without the tools for examining that complexity. The study of complexity requires a focus on change. We have to ask two fundamental questions about the world: why are things the way they are instead of a little bit different, and why are things the way they are instead of very different? The first is the question of self-regulation, of homeostasis, of the network of positive and negative feedbacks that absorb, transform, relocate and negate perturbations so that systems remain recognisably what they are despite the constant buffeting of opposing forces. It is the domain of systems theory proper, which takes a system as given and asks how it behaves.

The second is the question of evolution, history, development, of non-equilibrium theory. It starts from the simple proposition that things are the way they are because they got this way, not because they always were or have to be or will always be this way. The 'things' are both the objects of study and ourselves, the scientists who study them. The two questions are of course not independent. The long term processes create the variables of the persistent systems. The processes that keep aspects of systems intact also change other aspects and eventually change the identities and connections among the parts. The self-regulating processes not only preserve the equilibria but also the directions of change of equilibria. Equilibrium is itself a form of motion, a relatively stable relation among changing things. A dialectical viewpoint emphasises these aspects of historically developing and interacting processes.

At present science is being pulled in opposite directions. On the one hand, economic pressures are undermining the traditional relative autonomy of scientists, an autonomy which was always exaggerated but nonetheless real. The single minded concern of governments to cut costs and to privatise is shifting both control of science as a whole, and the conditions of work of scientists, to administrators. These administrators see science as an industry like any other industry and scientists as a scientific workforce to be managed like any other workforce. The product of the science industry is knowledge, knowledge that can become commodities either as physical objects or as services and reports. The economic rationality of the administrators encourages the fragmentation of scientific workshops, specialisation and short term, precisely defined goals. This situation also leads to decisions being based less on intellectual or social necessity and more on marketability and risk avoidance. They manage scientific labour with the familiar devices they use in any industry—a myopic view of 'efficiency', down-sizing, use of part-time and temporary researchers and teachers and hierarchical rankings that keep the producers divided. Scientists learn quickly to plan research efforts based on criteria of acceptability and fundability, to rush publication to meet the timetables of appointments and promotions, to weigh carefully the costs and benefits of sharing and secrecy.

These trends are in conflict with both the internal intellectual needs of science for a more integrated, dynamic, dialectical outlook and the urgent necessity of confronting problems too big to face in a fragmented way. A science that is up to the mark would differ from the traditional European and North American science in a number of ways:

1) It would be frankly partisan. I propose the hypothesis that all theories are wrong which promote, justify or tolerate injustice. The wrongness may be in the data, its interpretation or its application, but if we search for that wrongness we will also be led to truth.

2) It would be democratic in at least three ways. First, access to the sci-entific community would be open to everyone with the scientific vocation without the barriers of class, racism or misogyny. Second, the results of science would be available to the whole population in a form that is intelligible and without the secrecy often justified in the name of national security or proprietary rights. Third, it would recognise that science prospers when it can combine the knowledge and insights of institutional science with those of the farmers, patients, and inhabitants of workplaces and communities that make up the 'alternative' move-ments. This is not quite the same thing as combining professional and non-professional understanding, since alternative movements have always been invigorated by professionals who ally with them. The result would be a mobilisation of much more of the world's intelligence, cre-ativity and insight than ever before.

3) It must be polycentric. The centres of world science have shifted his-torically from the ancient Middle East, south and east Asia and Central America to Germany, France, England and now Europe and North America. This monopoly of knowledge has served monopolies of power. It has often resulted in the imposition of foreign agendas on the scientific communities of the Third World. It has also deprived us all of insights that are often less rigid, less fragmented and more dynamic, insights which arose in societies quite different from our own. Polycentric science must not become a sentimental orientalism or nationalism or def-erence to the ancient because it is ancient. Rather it must recognise that

each social context produces its own pattern of insight and blindness, its own urgencies and indifferences, its own penetrating revelations and built in confusions. A new global science must share techniques, knowledge and tools, be able to compare and choose, but also respectfully leave room for radically different approaches for facing the unknown.

4) It must be dialectical. The term dialectical materialism has had a bad reputation because of the way it was debased by Stalin and his school. The best dialecticians were eliminated or silenced, perhaps not singled out but caught up among others in a democracy of terror. It was then possible to reduce that rich perspective into a set of rigid rules and apologetics for decisions already taken on other grounds. However, as the most comprehensive self-conscious alternative to the predominant reductionism of Cartesian science, dialectical materialism has been the starting point for my own research. It offers the necessary emphasis on complexity, context, historicity, the interpenetration of seemingly mutually exclusive categories, the relative autonomy and mutual determination of different 'levels' of existence, and the contradictory, self-negating aspects of change.

5) It must be self-reflexive, recognising that those who intervene are also part of the system and that the way we approach the rest of nature must also be accounted for. Thus it has to be doubly historical, looking at the history of the objects of interest and of our understanding of those objects.

This is a programme that runs counter to the prevailing trends in science, education and technology. Therefore, it is not only an intellectual challenge but is also a highly political one which requires us to resist the pressures of the New World Order. When the world recovers from the confusion that has accompanied the euphoric globalisation of greed, when the certainties of the present moment are once again in doubt and our species joins together to continue its long quest for justice, equality, solidarity and now also survival, it is just possible that science will be there too, creating, receiving and sharing the knowledge that liberates.

Notes

1   The citation for the medal reads as follows: 'The Edinburgh Medal has been instituted by City of Edinburgh Council to honour men and women of science who have made a significant contribution to the understanding and wellbeing of humanity. It is awarded in 1996 to Richard Levins for his work on the integration of diverse sciences to create holistic models of population biology and ecosystem in practical co-operation with farmers and his life long commitment to science for the people.'

    Next year the Edinburgh International Science Festival will take place between 22 March and 6 April. More information about the festival can be obtained from EISF, 149 Rose Street, Edinburgh EH2 4LS (0131 220 3977).

The Babeuf bicentenary: conspiracy or revolutionary party?

IAN BIRCHALL

The year 1996 sees the 200th anniversary of Babeuf's short lived 'conspiracy for equality', an unsuccessful attempt to overthrow the moderate Directory, which governed France, and establish a society based on common ownership of property. Babeuf has long been recognised as an important precursor of the revolutionary socialist tradition; in the founding manifesto of the Communist International, Trotsky declared that the new organisation was 'carrying on in direct succession the heroic endeavours and martyrdom of a long line of revolutionary generations from Babeuf to Karl Liebknecht and Rosa Luxemburg'.[1]

Yet to English readers Babeuf remains a shadowy figure. Babeuf gets a name check in most histories of the French Revolution, but very little more. Only three book length studies have appeared in the course of the 20th century.[2] Partly this is a result of British parochialism, partly it is a result of Stalinism, which found it hard to reconcile the study of 'precursors' of Marxism with its attempt to transform Marxism into a quasi-religious doctrine. The most important work on Babeuf in the 20th century has been done by anti-Stalinist Marxists: Maurice Dommanget, a syndicalist who helped to arrange Trotsky's accommodation during his exile in France,[3] and Victor Dalin, a supporter of the Left Opposition in the 1920s who spent many years in labour camps.[4]

Babeuf's 'conspiracy' is often dismissed as futile or premature, and Babeuf himself seen as a utopian, a hangover from Jacobinism or a forerunner of Blanqui. The reality, however, is considerably more complex and more interesting. There is now a huge amount of information available on Babeuf which reveals him to be an original thinker and an organiser of considerable significance. The following account will concentrate on the episode of the 'conspiracy' and its political and organisational practice.[5]

Babeuf was born in 1760, in Picardy in north east France. He had no formal education,[6] but acquired a considerable amount of knowledge from his father, who was an army deserter turned taxman. Babeuf may even have learnt some Latin; certainly he always retained a deep enthusiasm for ancient Rome. Later on he was to adopt the forename 'Gracchus', after the Roman advocate of the 'agrarian law' (the redistribution of the land). As a teenager he spent a couple of years performing hard manual labour, working on the Picardy canal. Before the development of machinery, canal building required an army of thousands of labourers, and Babeuf was thus introduced to the wage earning working class which was beginning to emerge in France at this time. Then he became a *feudiste*, employed by landowners to search through documents in order to re-establish feudal rights. He claimed later that it was in the course of this work that he had discovered that the origins of private property, and hence of human inequality, lay in the violence and deception of the landowners.

Babeuf was an enthusiastic supporter of the French Revolution, from the storming of the Bastille through to the establishment of the Republic and the execution of the king. He was invariably on the side of the popular masses who wanted to take the revolution forward towards greater economic and political equality, and against those moderate elements who wanted to call a halt before their own privileges were destroyed. Until 1793 he spent most of his time in Picardy. His old profession had been made obsolete by the revolution, and instead he made several rather unsuccessful attempts to launch newspapers. He was also involved in a number of campaigns against unfair taxation.

In February 1793 he went to Paris, and found employment in the organisation that administered food supplies. Later that year he was jailed on a rather dubious charge of forgery dating back to his days in Picardy. He was released from prison in July 1794, just ten days after the fall of Robespierre and the Jacobins. The most radical phase of the revolution had been brought to an end by the moderate bourgeoisie, who wished to ensure that their own wealth and status were not threatened. But at the same time Robespierre had eroded his own support among the poorest sections of the Paris population; in particular the imposition of wage controls had alienated the emergent working class.

Initially Babeuf welcomed the fall of Jacobin rule. He had not been particularly sympathetic to Robespierre's most vigorous left wing critics, the so-called *enragés*, but as one who had a deep commitment to enriching democratic forms, he distrusted Robespierre's authoritarianism. In particular he was hostile to the repressive measures used during the civil war that had raged in the Vendée in western France.

Soon the realities of the new regime began to manifest themselves; the rich sought to line their own pockets while the poor faced increasing hardship. The well off flaunted their prosperity in luxury restaurants while the streets were full of starving people. The government was now in the hands of a five man Directory, and in Paris gangs of *muscadins* or 'gilded youth' emerged, bunches of thugs who launched physical attacks on the remaining groups of pro-Jacobins.

Babeuf had by this time launched a new paper, the *Tribun du Peuple* (*People's Tribune*). While the early issues were critical of the Jacobins, he did not hesitate long before recognising where the battle lines lay. His response to the strongarm tactics being used against the remaining Jacobins was quite unambiguous:

> If you want civil war, you can have it... You've cried 'To arms'. We've said the same to our people.[7]

Not surprisingly he soon found himself in jail again, and he spent most of 1795 locked up.

Babeuf was now vigorously opposed to the Directory, but he did not simply wish to revert to the period of Jacobin rule. He had developed a quite distinctive position which it is entirely legitimate to describe as 'socialist'. Of course the word 'socialist' was not yet in currency. Babeuf usually described his position as the advocacy of 'true equality' or 'common happiness'. But his aim of a society based on economic equality and common ownership of property is clearly recognisable as what later became known as socialism. Before 1789 Babeuf had been deeply influenced by the ideas of some of the 18th century utopian communists; during the revolution he had always combined activism with intensive reading and theoretical speculation.

Of course Babeuf did not think in terms of the distinction subsequently made by Marxists between 'bourgeois' and 'socialist' revolutions. His concern was always that the revolution should be continued to its logical conclusion, to fight against those who wished to stop it half way or roll back the gains already made. But his goal was quite clearly a society which would be based on economic as well as juridical equality, and which would therefore have no place for private property.

While in prison he had an extensive correspondence with Charles Germain, later to be one of the leaders of the 'conspiracy'. In one of his letters Babeuf set out a devastating critique of the market economy which has lost none of its power two centuries later:

> *Competition, far from aiming at perfection, submerges conscientiously made products under a mass of deceptive goods contrived to dazzle the public, competition which achieves low prices only by obliging the worker to waste his skill in botched work, by starving him, by destroying his moral standards through lack of scruples; competition gives the victory only to whoever has most money; competition, after the struggle, ends up simply with a monopoly in the hands of the winner and the withdrawal of low prices; competition which manufactures any way it likes, at random, and runs the risk of not finding any buyers and destroying a large amount of raw material which could have been used usefully but which will no longer be good for anything.*[8]

Some historians concede that Babeuf personally had developed a socialist position, but claim that his following came only from those nostalgic for the good old days of Robespierre when they were better fed. Obviously any political movement will be perceived in different ways by different sections of its audience, according to their degree of political sophistication. But the *Analysis of Babeuf's Doctrine*, which was widely distributed as a leaflet and flyposted all over Paris, contains a pretty clear statement of Babeuf's fundamental position:

> ●*Nature has given every man an equal right to enjoy all goods.*
> ●*The aim of society is to defend this equality, often attacked by the strong and wicked in the state of nature, and to increase, by the co-operation of all, the common enjoyments.*
> ●*...There is oppression when one person is exhausted by work and lacks everything, while another wallows in abundance without doing anything.*
> ●*No-one can, without committing a crime, appropriate to his exclusive possession the fruits of the earth or of industry.*
> ●*In a true society, there must be neither rich nor poor.*

On leaving jail on 12 October 1795, Babeuf faced the fundamental problem of how to pursue his socialist goal and at the same time relate to the immediate situation of crisis he saw around him. For Babeuf the policies of the Directory were not only reactionary in themselves, but opened the door to a much more sinister danger. Royalist plotting was intensifying, while among the common people many were beginning to wonder whether the whole revolutionary experience had been worthwhile. The danger of a monarchist coup which would overthrow the Republic and destroy all the gains of the revolution was a very real threat. If the Directory was not overthrown from the left then there was a good chance it would be overthrown from the right. The Directory was performing a perilous balancing act between Royalists and Republicans, but at any moment it might lose its balance.

To respond to such a situation, organisation was necessary. Over the previous couple of years, especially when he was in prison, Babeuf had gathered together a tiny nucleus of like minded revolutionaries (paradoxically the prisons provided a means of bringing opponents of the regime together). Notable among them were Buonarroti, an Italian disciple of Rousseau who had served the revolutionary government in Corsica and had become a French citizen; Sylvain Maréchal, a poet and militant atheist who had devised an early version of the revolutionary calendar; and Charles Germain, a professional soldier since the age of 17, deeply influenced by both 18th century materialism and the Anabaptists.[9]

In the autumn of 1795 various critics of the regime had attempted to revive the Jacobin tradition of revolutionary clubs by setting up the Panthéon Club. This met in a former religious building close to the Panthéon in what is now the Latin Quarter (just down the road from the area where the first barricades went up in the rebellion of 1968). Often the members met sitting on the floor in a basement by torchlight. Babeuf, Buonarroti and others participated in these meetings. By February 1796 the Directory decided that the club must be closed down. A young general who was rapidly making a name for himself, Bonaparte, took personal responsibility for the operation.

Babeuf now faced a difficult choice between different ways forward. He himself was clearly a socialist. But he did not have enough co-thinkers to engage in anything other than the most abstract propaganda. He had been writing a book to be entitled *Equality*; if he had completed it, he would have been listed among the utopian communists of the late 18th century, known only to specialists of the esoteric. Alternatively he could have trailed along with the ex-Jacobins, anxious to turn the clock back to the golden days of Robespierre. In that event his distinctive contribution would have been totally submerged.

The significance of Babeuf is that he accepted neither of these alternatives, but strove for a solution which overcame the dilemma. He made no secret of his socialist ideas, and put them forward in his mass propaganda; but he also accepted the necessity of working with, and attempting to mobilise, those whose ideas did not go beyond Robespierre's. In particular, Babeuf and his supporters used as one of their agitational demands the restoration of the Jacobin Constitution of 1793. This had included the defence of the right to property. Babeuf and his associates did not conceal their criticism of this point, but at the same time saw the appeal to the 1793 Constitution as one which could rally the masses of common people in Paris. Here we see Babeuf grappling with two problems that have returned, in different forms, for revolutionaries of later generations: how to make alliances that will be effective in practice without compromising the basic goals of the movement; and how to relate short term demands that win popular support to the long term perspective of social transformation.

Thus was born the 'conspiracy for equality'. Before going any further it is necessary to clarify the use of the term conspiracy. When Babeuf and his associates were put on trial in 1797, the main charge used against them was that of conspiracy, a charge to be used repeatedly against socialists and trade unionists for the following two centuries. And when, in 1828, Buonarroti published his influential history of the events, he gave it the title *Babeuf's Conspiracy For Equality*. So we seem to be stuck with the term (even though it is a notoriously slippery one that meant quite different things to state prosecutors and to revolutionary activists).

But it is important not to jump from the word to a notion of conspiracy that involves a tiny group operating secretly and manipulatively behind the backs of the masses. Nothing could be further from the reality of the activity of Babeuf. Indeed, when the state prosecutor at Babeuf's trial in Vendôme began his case against the alleged 'conspirators', he described their methods as follows:

> *Their means were the publication and distribution of anarchistic newspapers, writings and pamphlets...the formation of a multitude of little clubs run by their agents; it was the establishment of organisers and flyposters; it was the corrupting of workshops; it was the infernal art of sowing false rumours and spreading false news, of stirring up the people by blaming the government for all the ills resulting from current circumstances.[10]*

Such activity scarcely conforms to the common notion of 'conspiracy'; indeed much of it will seem remarkably familiar to most readers of this journal.

Certainly the organisation adopted a semi-clandestine structure; this was necessitated by the degree of political repression prevailing under the Directory. For example, the advocacy of the 1793 Constitution was punishable by death and indeed it was for this advocacy that Babeuf and Darthé were executed after the jury had thrown out the conspiracy charges.

At the centre of the organisation was a committee of seven men, including Babeuf, Buonarroti and Maréchal. 'Agents' (full time organisers) were appointed for each of the 12 *arrondissements* of Paris. However, the agents were not to know each other's identities, and neither were they to know who was on the secret central committee (though of course Babeuf himself, who was living in hiding, was publicly identified with the organisation). Instead an 'intermediate agent' was to have responsibility for all communication between the agents and the centre. In theory the 'intermediate agent' was not supposed to know the content or significance of the communications he was carrying; in fact he was an experienced political activist and almost certainly knew what he was doing.

Many historians have tried to see the centralisation of the Babeuf organisation as a sinister forerunner of Leninism—and hence of Stalinism. There is little substance to this claim. The basic principle was that no member of the organisation should know more than was necessary for the exercise of their particular functions. It is a principle that is no more than common sense in any situation where an organisation is likely to be subject to infiltration, and where individuals risk interrogation. If it is a principle that has been applied by Leninist parties in certain conditions, it is also one that has been used by a wide range of political organisations under conditions of repression—for example resistance movements in the Second World War.

A vigorous correspondence was maintained between the centre and the agents; circulars were sent out almost daily, and regular reports were received back from the agents. Of course everything had to be copied by hand, and Babeuf himself did copying work amid his many other tasks.

The 'conspirators' were guilty of one serious lapse of security. Copies of all outgoing and incoming correspondence were carefully stored—and seized by the authorities at the time of Babeuf's arrest. They were subsequently published in two large volumes and used as the basis of the prosecution case against Babeuf at the Vendôme trial to show just how dangerous the conspiracy had been.[11] Babeuf's heirs would be well advised to learn the lesson and invest in a paper-shredder—but historians can scarcely regret the mistake since the documents provide us with an incomparable source that enables us to get a real sense of just how the conspiracy worked.

The role of the agents was central to the whole organisation. They received a small payment—the equivalent of a worker's wage. In return the centre's expectations were high. If the agents did not carry out their duties adequately they received stinging rebukes and, in at least one case, threats. A dilatory agent received a letter with the ominous conclusion: 'Remember that what you were told in your first instruction is still valid: "our only loss would be you, and even if you were ill intentioned, you could not harm us".'[12]

But generally the agents seem to have worked well. Their relation with the centre was a two way process. They were given instructions, but also asked to report regularly on the circumstances in their districts. Some of the information required was of direct practical relevance—for example the location of arms stores. But the crucial task of the agents was to report on the 'thermometer of opinion'—that is, the state of consciousness among the common people in their areas. There are reports of disputes in shops and snatches of conversation overheard in the streets—all designed to give an impression of the popular mood. Far from going behind the backs of the people, the conspirators knew that they could only have any success by relating to the feelings and attitudes of the common people.

Moreover, the job of the agents was not to substitute themselves for the masses, but rather to facilitate popular organisation. They were told to 'multiply small meetings as much as you can'. To avoid the dangers of infiltration these were to be held in private homes rather than cafes. Most importantly, a large number of small meetings was to be preferred to bringing too many people together at the same time.[13]

The whole operation was run on a shoestring; if agents were given expenses, it was grudgingly and with the reminder: 'Be aware that this revolution is not undertaken by aristocrats, and if it were, you wouldn't want to serve it...the only funds come from the contributions of *sans-culottes*'.[14]

Of course, a newspaper was central to the organisation of the conspiracy. Babeuf's *Tribun du Peuple* had existed well before the conspiracy came into existence, but the last issues were put at the service of the organisation. Indeed, Babeuf always saw his paper as an organiser rather than simply a journalistic enterprise.

The circulation of the *Tribun du Peuple* was probably around 2,000. Undoubtedly it played a key role in diffusing Babeuf's ideas and giving an analysis of the contemporary situation. Some historians have used the subscription list of the journal to give an account of the nature of Babeuf's popular support.[15] This is, however, an unreliable source. The *Tribun du Peuple* was a theoretical journal, often difficult to understand for those unversed in political debate. Moreover, it was expensive. Naturally enough it was the better off, more educated supporters of the conspiracy who subscribed to the journal. The poor artisans and wage workers, who constituted Babeuf's natural target audience, were often too poor to subscribe and were sometimes illiterate. Among soldiers, who were another key section of the audience, the situation was even worse: one estimate is that among the troops, largely of peasant origin, who were stationed in Paris, only 10 percent could read and write. Moreover, not all subscriptions were individual; it was a common practice for political newspapers to be read aloud in inns and lemonade shops, so the ideas had a wider currency than crude subscription data would suggest.

However, because of the limitations on the *Tribun du Peuple*, Babeuf recognised the necessity for other forms of propaganda. Alongside the

Tribun du Peuple another paper was launched in the spring of 1796, namely *L'Eclaireur (The Scout)*. This was written in a much more popular style, and rather than pursuing theoretical analysis it aimed at radical exposure journalism. Thus the luxurious lifestyle of the members of the Directory was exposed—for example, when each member of the Directory was having eight dozen specially embroidered handkerchiefs made. And the paper took an interest in a high official called Merlin who was reported to have several 'nymphs' from the Opéra as his mistresses.

An even wider audience was reached with flyposting. The use of posters had been widespread during the revolution, but Babeuf's supporters used them to particular effect. The authorities recognised the danger and constantly had them removed, but the reports from the agents show how successful the activity was. Thus in the second *arrondissement* a policeman tore down a poster, but was immediately confronted by an 'energetic patriot' who said: 'Rogue, you have come to rob the people of the truth which we want them to know; you are an agent of those who are starving us.' At this, the readers of the poster applauded and the policeman had to run for his life.[16] In the seventh *arrondissement* some 2,000 people were said to have queued up to read a poster addressed to soldiers.[17]

Another method of propagating ideas even among the illiterate was the use of songs. A focal point for that activity was a cafe known as the 'Chinese Baths', where Sophie Lapierre won an audience for the ideas of the conspiracy. Lapierre had been a school teacher and an embroiderer; she was tried at Vendôme and behaved with the utmost courage, refusing to recognise the legitimacy of the court and leading the prisoners in song in defiance of the judges. While the songs did not have a high degree of political sophistication, they made the basic point about human equality in vivid fashion. For example:

Benevolent Mother Nature
You created us to be equal!
So why the murderous inequality
Of property and of work?
Awake to the sound of our voice
Come forth out of the dark night
People! Take back your rights
The sun shines for everyone.[18]

Another of the tasks of the agents was to compile contact lists—lists of all the 'patriots' in their area who might be sympathetic to the aims of the conspiracy and who could be called on for action. The lists that survived are often of a remarkable frankness, showing no illusions in the political sophistication of those referred to. Thus one list names 'the

Fleurie brothers, horse dealers, living near the market, excellent in a fight and that's all'.[19] In another case a certain Himbert was described as an 'ardent and courageous patriot', fit for a position of command, but the agent warned that due to his excitable temperament he should not be informed of his role till the last moment.[20]

But while it was necessary to be honest about the potential of contacts, the aim was always to draw them in rather than to create barriers; a letter to the agent of the sixth *arrondissement* in Babeuf's own hand states: 'If people are still susceptible to conversion, it is better to win them over than to reject them from our ranks, because in that way we increase our party and diminish that of our opponents'.[21]

More prosperous supporters were, of course, not neglected; a circular to agents tells them: 'You will encourage…well-off patriots to contribute towards the enormous printing costs that revolutionaries are obliged to bear'.[22] A variety of talented people were attracted by the movement; among Babeuf's sympathisers was Valentin Haüy, a pioneer of education for the blind and the original inventor of the system of printing now known as braille.

The whole purpose of the work of the agents was to ensure that the conspiracy was rooted in the various localities. Certainly there is some evidence that Babeuf was popular among the common people in some districts. A letter from Babeuf's elder son, Emile, aged only ten but active in organising the conspiracy, tells how he went into a shop to buy some medicine and when he told the shopkeeper he was Babeuf's son, she cut one third off the price.[23]

Daniel Guérin, following Dommanget, has argued that Babeuf should have concentrated more exclusively on working class struggles.[24] To have done so would have condemned Babeuf to mere propagandism; the working class alone was still too small to challenge the Directory. Only an alliance of wage workers and other *sans-culottes* could have any hope of making an impact.

But it is also important to recognise that there was a substantial working class in Paris in the 1790s, and that Babeuf and his supporters did make every effort to relate to it. As well as large numbers of market porters (who had on one occasion saved Babeuf from arrest by hurling mud and rubbish at a policeman who was pursuing him) and dockers (Paris was at this time a major port), there were a number of quite substantial factories and workshops, a few employing hundreds of workers, many employing more than 20 or 30.

The agents were particularly instructed to examine conditions and attitudes in the workshops in their areas. The results are somewhat mixed. In the 12th *arrondissement* the agent reported that there was little potential at the Gobelins tapestry factory, which employed around 100 workers. As was often the case with the luxury industries, workers were afraid that any attack on the privileged classes who bought their products would mean a fall in sales. But the agent also found a dye works with some 30 workers, and about 20 tanneries with between 15 and 50 workers each, where the prospects were rather more hopeful.[25] The same agent reported that there was growing unemployment, which was making more workers think of the Robespierre period as one of greater prosperity. The agent of the eighth *arrondissement* reported on a wage dispute where an employer had given his workers a rise to cover the falling value of paper money, but had in fact not compensated them adequately.[26] Thus, while it would be quite wrong to claim that the Babeuf conspiracy was a specifically proletarian movement, it would also be wrong to ignore how relevant wage workers were to it.

Mention should also be made of the role of women in the conspiracy. Babeuf had long been sensitive to the fact of women's oppression; as early as 1786 he had written a long letter analysing the roots of this oppression.[27] In a reply to the agent of the eighth *arrondissement* the central committee wrote: 'We know the influence that can be exercised by this interesting sex, who do not bear the yoke of tyranny any more indifferently than we do, and who are no less courageous when it comes to taking action to break it'.[28]

A number of women played a key role in the conspiracy, including Sophie Lapierre and Babeuf's wife, Marie-Anne-Victoire Longlet, who had responsibility for distribution of the *Tribun du Peuple*. Several women were put on trial at Vendôme; all were acquitted, though one contemporary report tells how after the verdict Charles Germain gloated that the jury had been duped, for it had been the women who encouraged the men.[29]

The conspiracy centred on Paris, but considerable work was done to ensure support on a national level. Recent research by Jean-Marc Schiappa has shown that the conspiracy had an extensive network of supporters in various regions of the country, notably in Babeuf's home territory of Picardy, and in the Mediterranean south.[30]

The conspiracy also devoted great attention to agitation within the army, recognising that unless the soldiers could be drawn over to the side of the revolutionary forces, any rising would be crushed. Prospects for support looked encouraging. Since the heroic days of the defence of the Republic a couple of years earlier, the morale of the army had fallen catastrophically, a situation which was most clearly expressed in a massive level of desertions. One of Babeuf's supporters reported that most soldiers stationed in Paris would 'gladly swap the Republic for a cake from their home village'.[31]

Another report gave a vivid account of the miseries of military life and the grievances of soldiers:

> The soldier...is today not only dying of hunger, but he has no shoes and no clothes; he can't have his shirt laundered, because that costs 30 francs, and where would he get them?...he is also annoyed, vexed and crushed under a heap of tortures graced with the name of **military discipline**, and at bottom it is a tyranny which is much more highly perfected than under the noble ministers of Louis XVI.[32]

The conspirators made great efforts to win support in the army. Much of the propaganda material aimed at soldiers was carefully written in colloquial, earthy language, full of obscenities, designed to appeal to the military: 'We're fucked, my poor friend..., yes, we're fucked and flat broke if we swallow the pill they've shoved in our gobs'.[33] A poster called 'Soldier Stop And Read' urged, 'No! Citizen soldiers! You will not shoot at your brothers...'[34]

At the end of April the Police Legion mutinied. This was a body organised by Bonaparte to ensure security in the capital. Its members were recruited from the Parisian popular classes and many of its soldiers were profoundly hostile to the Directory. But Babeuf's supporters were not strong enough to generalise the movement. The rising was crushed and 17 militant soldiers were shot.

Detailed plans continued to be made for the insurrection. Banners and pennants were planned; snipers were organised and arrangements were made to seize food stores and the National Treasury; it was planned that all property in pawnshops would be handed back to its owners, a measure designed to win great support among the poor. Buonarroti claimed there were 17,000 men ready for the insurrection.[35] But it was not to be. A government informer, Grisel, had made his way into the organisation, and the conspirators, quite correctly anxious to welcome and make use of a man who seemed well informed and influential in the army, were too open in the way they received him and allowed him to gain information.

On 10 May 1796 the police arrested Babeuf and Buonarroti, seizing documents and arms. The following year the main conspirators were put on trial at Vendôme. The trial lasted 14 weeks, and Babeuf and his friends fought like cats every single day, exploiting every legal technicality and being deliberately disruptive into the bargain. Only with the greatest difficulty did the prosecution persuade the jury to convict, and even then a number of leading activists were acquitted. Only two death sentences were passed, on Babeuf and Darthé. Several others were imprisoned, among them Buonarroti, who survived into the 1830s and wrote a history of the conspiracy which inspired a whole generation of new militants in the period before 1848.

Thus it can be seen that Babeuf's 'conspiracy' was far from what might be imagined as a conspiratorial organisation. In no way was it the predecessor of Che Guevara's peasant armies or the Baader-Meinhof gang. On the contrary, Babeuf firmly rejected acts of terrorism. In his evidence at Vendôme, the traitor Grisel was obliged to admit that, when as a provocation, he had proposed setting fire to castles outside Paris as a diversion during the planned insurrection, Babeuf had firmly rejected the suggestion. Babeuf had likewise refused an offer by an army officer to assassinate the five members of the Directory.[36]

Likewise, the conspirators were well aware of the dangers of excessive clandestinity; in a letter to the agent of the 12th *arrondissement*, they wrote:

> *As far as possible, you should distribute publications in a direct manner. You have to show a bit of daring if you want to encourage it in others; clandestine methods inspire distrust in the uneducated masses. They think that if you seem to be smuggling your ideas in, then there must be something reprehensible about them.*[37]

Any serious revolutionary organisation has to strike a balance between secrecy and openness, after making a careful analysis of the objective conditions it has to work under. The basic principle must be as much security as necessary, as much openness as possible. Of course Babeuf and friends, like most organisations since, did not always get it right. Certainly they made mistakes about security, and in the case of Grisel they made a fatal one. But the mistakes were made because they were anxious to open up the organisation to potential recruits. An organisation that does not take risks may survive, but it is unlikely to grow. Some historians have sneered at the conspiracy, saying it was widely infiltrated with police agents. But if that was true, then why did the prosecution at Vendôme find it necessary to stake so much on the testimony of a single witness, the informer Grisel?

Babeuf and his comrades were grappling with real problems, with very little historical experience to help them. If subsequent revolutionaries have been able to learn from their mistakes, it is because they were the real mistakes of a real movement. And, as well as planning the details of their organisation, the conspirators also spent much time drawing up the details of a future society based on the principles of true equality. Buonarroti gives an extensive account of these in his history.

What is striking here is just how far Babeuf's vision of a future society diverged from that of Rousseau and most 18th century utopians. Contrary to the claims of many critics, Babeuf was not an 'economic pessimist' who believed the only hope for equality was to share misery equally among all. Babeuf was no ascetic, and the word 'abundance' recurs frequently in his writings. Buonarroti records that the conspiracy aimed '...to provide in superabundance things which are necessary to all, and to provide them with objects of pleasure which are not condemned by public morality'.[38]

The draft economic decree produced by the secret Directory promised that the new society would provide everyone with healthy, comfortable and decently furnished accommodation, clothing, laundry, heat and light, adequate food—bread, meat, poultry, fish, eggs—and wine, as well as a free health service.[39]

Likewise Babeuf and his associates anticipated Marx in advocating the transcendence of the distinction between town and country. They envisaged a network of villages, linked by roads and canals so that communication became easier. In their draft 'economic decree' the conspirators gave special attention to the development of telegraphic communication. (This was not, of course, electric telegraphy but a form of semaphore signalling, perfected by Chappe in 1794.)[40]

Far from opposing technological progress, as Rousseau did, the conspirators recognised that a socialist society would use technology to full advantage:

> *It is only within a system based on community that the use of machines would be of true benefit to humanity, by reducing toil while increasing the abundance of necessary and agreeable objects. Today, by suppressing a great quantity of manual labour, they take bread out of the mouths of a large number of men, in the interest of a few insatiable speculators whose profits they increase.*[41]

Of course, with the massive benefit of 200 years hindsight to help us, we can see that Babeuf's conspiracy was doomed to failure. Engels was correct, if somewhat uncharitable, to describe the conspiracy as 'insane...Babeuf's attempt to jump from the Directorate immediately into communism'.[42] Even in the unlikely event of the insurrection having succeeded, it would at best have ushered in a second period of Jacobin rule, which would probably have been even more short lived than that of 1793-1794. The objective conditions for any kind of socialism quite simply did not exist, and would not exist for several decades to come.

Yet it is one thing to make a historical analysis of the reasons for Babeuf's failure; it is quite a different one to adopt the complacent and patronising attitude that dismisses the whole episode as futile, that says that, if Babeuf had known what we know now, he would not have done what he did but would have stayed in bed. We know what we know precisely because Babeuf and others like him did what they did.

After the defeat of the conspiracy there was a prolonged downturn in resistance. A few of Babeuf's followers reappear in later brief opposition movements, but with the rise of Napoleon the left was crushed for a generation. Yet in the longer term Babeuf provided a vital source of ideas and inspiration for the rising socialist movement. Without the heritage of Babeuf, Marx and Engels would have had greater difficulty in achieving what they did.

François Furet has revived a well worn argument in seeing a continuity from Babeuf through Blanqui to Lenin. He tells us that Babeuf's alleged voluntarism,

> ...is the highest peak of the revolutionary belief that political will can do everything. The last wave of Jacobin extremism—and doubtless the only intellectual synthesis of the egalitarian passion of those times—elaborates here the theory of the revolutionary putsch, essential for the understanding of the 19th and 20th centuries. The history of secret societies in Europe after the Treaty of Vienna has its origin here, as well as the Russian revolutionary tradition from populism to Bolshevism.[43]

The reality is rather more complex. As far as Blanqui, the greatest of the French leaders of secret societies, is concerned, it appears that he knew relatively little of Babeuf. Blanqui conforms far more than Babeuf to the typical stereotype of the 'conspirator'; he had far less sense of the practicalities of mass propaganda and agitation. Blanqui was a revolutionary of enormous courage and total integrity, but in organisational terms he marks a regression from Babeuf's achievement.

Bolshevism is a different matter again. Contrary to right wing mythology, there is no single 'Leninist' theory of the party; Lenin's organisational philosophy made massive shifts between 1902, 1905, 1908, 1912 and 1917, according to his evaluation of objective conditions. In fact there seems to be little evidence that Lenin knew anything of Babeuf; there is a total of two cursory references to Babeuf in his entire writings. But if there is a link between Babeuf and Lenin, then I hope to have shown in this article that Babeuf is the forerunner of the Lenin who urged the opening up of the party in 1905,[44] not the imaginary conspiratorial Lenin of right wing fantasy.

A careful reading of the available documentation about Babeuf shows him to be an original thinker and a talented organiser, whose early death doubtless prevented the full flowering of his promise. There is much in the documentation of the conspiracy, from the general concern to unite theory and practice, down to details of such activities as flyposting, that will seem familiar to revolutionaries two centuries later. Babeuf is very much a part of our tradition.

Notes

1   J Degras (ed), *The Communist International*, I (London, 1971), p47.
2   E Belfort Bax, *The Last Episode of the French Revolution* (London, 1911); D Thomson, *The Babeuf Plot* (London, 1947); R B Rose, *Gracchus Babeuf* (Stanford, 1978). The first two are very dated; Rose's book is sound and sympathetic, but limited in its political understanding.
3   P Broué, *Trotsky* (Paris, 1988), p794.
4   Dalin was a signatory of the pro-Trotskyist statement by members of the Communist Youth, published as Appendix IV in L Trotsky, *The New Course* (Ann Arbor, 1965), pp114-118.
5   For a full treatment of Babeuf's life and thought see I H Birchall, *The Spectre of Babeuf* (Macmillan, 1997).
6   Socialists defend state education, but we should not fetishise schooling; at least two great revolutionaries, Babeuf and Victor Serge, never went to school.
7   *Tribun du Peuple*, No 30.
8   Babeuf, *Ecrits*, ed C Mazauric (Paris, 1988), p258.
9   A religious movement of the early 16th century, inspired by Thomas Münzer, which advocated equality and common ownership of property.
10   *Haute-Cour de Justice: Exposé Fait par les Accusateurs Nationaux* (Paris, 1797), p23.
11   *Copie des Pièces Saisies* (Paris, 1797). The material was arranged in bundles and documents, and referred to by number—eg 7/27 would be the 27th item in the seventh bundle.
12   Ibid, 21/11.
13   Ibid, 7/89.
14   Ibid, 16/11. *Sans-culotte*—the word literally means those who did not wear (couldn't afford) the knee-breeches worn by the upper and middle classes—was a term used to refer to the section of the urban population that worked and was poor, ie shopkeepers and artisans as well as wage workers.
15   For example A Soboul, 'Sectional personnel and Babouvist personnel' in *Understanding the French Revolution* (London, 1988).
16   *Copie des Pièces Saisies*, 20/8.
17   Ibid, 22/17.
18   Ibid, 15/4.
19   Ibid, 10/17.
20   Ibid, 20/2.
21   Ibid, 16/9.
22   Ibid, 7/93.
23   Ibid, 8/4.
24   D Guérin, *La Lutte de Classes sous la Première Règublique*, II (Paris, 1968), p401; in general Guérin is a little harsh on Babeuf, and some of his tactical criticisms can be seen as sectarian; but this should not detract from the original and perceptive contribution Guérin made to the understanding of the revolution.
25   *Copie des Pièces Saisies*, 10/25.
26   Ibid, 10/24, 14/2.
27   *Oeuvres de Babeuf* I (Paris, 1977), pp91-102; the same was not true of all his associates. In 1801 Sylvain Maréchal was to argue that women should not be allowed to learn to read!

28 *Copie des Pièces Saisies*, 14/20.
29 *Mémoires du Comte Dufort de Cheverny*, II (Paris, 1909), p267.
30 J-M Schiappa, *Gracchus Babeuf avec les Egaux* (Paris, 1991), pp135-146.
31 *Copie des Pièces Saisies*, 3/3.
32 Ibid, 10/19.
33 Buonarroti, *La Conspiration pour l'Egalité*, II (Paris, 1957), p108.
34 Ibid, II, p79.
35 Ibid, I, p145.
36 *Débats du procès*, II (Paris, 1797), pp90-91, 102-103.
37 *Copie des Pièces Saisies*, 14/19.
38 Buonarroti, I, p158.
39 Ibid, II, p208.
40 Ibid, I, pp165-166, II, p210.
41 Ibid, I, p159.
42 Marx and Engels, *Collected Works*, XXV (London, 1987), pp609-610.
43 F Furet and M Ozouf, *Dictionnaire Critique de la Révolution Française* (Paris, 1988), pp204-205.
44 '...rally all the worker Social-Democrats round yourselves, incorporate them in the ranks of the party organisations by hundreds and thousands.' V I Lenin, *Collected Works*, vol X (Moscow 1962), p32.

A voice for the poor

A review of Christopher Hill, **Liberty Against the Law: Some Seventeenth-Century Controversies** *(Penguin Press, 1996), £25*

BRIAN MANNING

There was much talk of 'law' and 'liberty' during the English Revolution of 1640-60, but Christopher Hill in his new book asks the questions 'whose law?' and 'whose liberty?' The law was made in parliament by big landowners, with a few wealthy merchants; it was administered by judges and lawyers drawn from well-to-do families, themselves landowners, and by juries composed of lesser property owners. But most of the population owned little or no property. During the 16th and 17th centuries in England 'the poor' included more than 'the casual victims of misfortune or old age'. 'The poor' became 'a substantial proportion of the population' and 'a permanent class with no hope of escape from their poverty'. Driven from access to the land and its resources they became paupers, vagabonds or wage labourers: 'By the end of the 17th century life-long wage labourers were probably a majority of the population.' 'The poor' were not represented in parliament, they had no share in making legislation but 'were legislated against', and the function of the law was to protect property, secure liberty for property owners and keep 'the poor' in order. The law was not their law, nor was liberty their liberty.

'The poor' are the subject of Hill's book. He seeks to recover from the literature of the period—plays, ballads, pamphlets—what may have been their views and attitudes. He maintains that playwrights may occasionally give accurate expression to the outlook of the lower classes, that ballads may 'give us the history which commoners knew, history from the commoners' point of view', and that during the revolution 'pam-

phlets written by people with no university education—by women even',
may make public for the first time the opinions of some of the populace.

This is a highly desirable enterprise and it is executed ingeniously and
deftly. Hill shows his great skill in finding hitherto unsuspected relation-
ships between different phenomena and in drawing out new meanings by
cross-referencing numerous writings. Nevertheless, his evidence is
inevitably drawn to a large extent from people who were outside the
groups whose views he seeks to recover. Some historians will query the
validity of his method and whether his sources do reveal the outlook of
what he agrees to be an 'inarticulate' and 'silent' majority. This attitude
gives such historians an excuse to avoid the questions which Hill asks,
and it is worth noting that all he claims for his book is that it raises some
questions. His provisional answers give a voice to 'the poor' of 17th
century England, and I am persuaded that it is an authentic voice.

Hill's hypothesis is that various groups among 'the poor', some small,
others large, saw 'the law' as the enemy of 'freedom', and sought
freedom from 'the law'. Vagabonds (estimated to number 80,000 in the
early 17th century) were 'masterless men'—and women—of no settled
abode, following the open road, living by begging and stealing, outside
society and its settled family and household structures, free from control
by the church and the state—until they were caught and punished. They
had an independence and a freedom of sorts, more than the landless
peasants who remained in their villages. Some literature romanticised
them, but Hill comments:

> In real life I do not suppose that many people chose to be beggars, then as
> now. But the open road and the greenwood offered more romantic possibili-
> ties than today's city pavements. Politicians and pamphleteers who had
> themselves never to face beggary, then as now, portrayed them as idle
> scroungers. Those whose unemployment and begging had been forced upon
> them had to make the best of a bad job. I suspect that plays and ballads in
> praise of a beggar's life were not often composed by beggars.

Pirates and highwaymen carved out areas of freedom from and
against the law, and could achieve heroic status in popular eyes. Hill
gives a fascinating account of pirate crews as partners in co-operative
enterprises. They were not wage earners under a hierarchic structure of
authority, but shared the risks and the profits in an egalitarian and democratic milieu: 'Captains were often elected, and were answerable to their
crews; decisions on policy and disciplinary punishments were democra-
tically taken.'

Whereas pirates operated in collectives, highwaymen were individuals, often ex-soldiers and runaway apprentices (there were also

highwaywomen). The literature which depicted them as 'gentlemen of the road' taking from the rich and giving to the poor, as in the popular legend of Robin Hood, may have reflected or influenced their behaviour. Smugglers and poachers provided valued services for their neighbours, who did not respect the laws against their activities. Piracy, highway robbery, smuggling and poaching were all strategies developed by the impoverished to survive without submitting to the discipline of full time wage labour increasingly being imposed by the advance of capitalism.

The main arena of conflict, however, was between the law imposed by the ruling class and the customs of traditional rural communities. 'Freedom' for the mass of poor peasants 'meant living according to traditional customary rules, accepted unquestioningly from time immemorial'. Struggles occurred over enclosures, which were pushed through by landlords and the bigger peasant farmers, and backed by the law. Customary rights to access to common lands, forests and wastes were extinguished. The poorest were thus deprived of ancient rights to have pasture for a few sheep or cows, to dig peat or take wood, and to collect nuts and berries. They lost an important part of their subsistence, which had enabled them to be at least partly free from dependence on wage labour. Now they were forced to become full time wage workers: 'The law in the 17th century aimed at turning the mass of the peasantry off the soil and forcing them into wage labour to produce wealth for their employers and their country, though not for themselves.' The series of game laws passed by parliaments from the 14th to the 18th century also exemplified the conflict between law and custom. Villagers were deprived of what they regarded as traditional customary rights and hunting was made a monopoly of the landowners and a badge of their class. Resistance by means of poaching was an aspect of class struggle between peasants and landowners.

Hill regards the English Revolution as 'a turning point'. He illustrates this by reference to the abolition of feudal tenures and the Court of Wards by the victorious parliamentarians at the end of the civil war, an act confirmed after the Restoration of the monarchy in 1660. He rightly says that the importance of this has been 'unaccountably neglected by historians'. It relieved large landowners from costs to their estates when the heir was a minor and from dependence on royal favour to avoid the worst consequences of such a minority; it made them absolute owners, less dependent on the crown, and more disposed to make long term capital investments to integrate their estates into the growing capitalist market economy. He notes the increased severity of the game laws after the Restoration and the taming of the religious dissenters who had been at the heart of the defeated radical revolution. He describes the struggles against enclosures, the dispossession of poorer peasants and the growth of full time wage labour, as central to the transition to capitalism. However, he does not consider whether the Revolution removed obstacles to these developments and accelerated them. His study is confined largely to the poor and how they coped during the period of transition; it is not intended to be a study of the Revolution as a turning point. However, struggles for freedom from the law do impinge upon the Revolution, a point which Hill occasionally makes clear but does not explore.

In several previous works Hill has explained the failure and defeat of the radicals in the Revolution; now he turns to the mass of the poor and their defeat by the ruling class in their struggles for freedom from the law. On this his conclusion is important:

> *Potential supporters of freedom from the law, or those whose self-interest should have led them to support freedom, were almost certainly a majority of the population. But they were unorganised outside their communities, perhaps unorganisable except in moments of extreme crisis; and they had no conception of politics apart from what had traditionally existed, and myths of a freer past.*

Some of them fall into the categories of Eric Hobsbawm's 'primitive rebels' and 'social bandits'.

Hill's social framework is loose, but the fluidity in the social structure at the time of his study provides some justification for this. Sometimes he speaks of 'the permanent poor', sometimes of an 'underclass', also sometimes of a 'sub-class', and sometimes of a 'proletariat'. He extends his social framework upwards by including separatists from the Church of England, who 'felt that the worship enjoined by the state church was contrary to the Gospel' and broke the law 'in order to be free to worship as they believed God demanded'. These people do not fit easily with the other groups which impress me as forming the main thrust of his study because they were not driven by want or seeking to preserve customary rights, and they were ideologically more sophisticated. However, in view of my earlier comments I cannot object to them being there because they had the clearest link with the revolutionary struggles of the mid-17th century.

Christopher Hill always relates the past to the present. His refrain 'liberty for whom to do what?' resonates from the 17th century to the end of the 20th, and remains the key to unlocking the class nature of the state and society. A main theme of his book is the struggle against wage labour, and although some historians may think that he exaggerates popular hostility to wage labour, I think he has made his case. He notes that the wage earners eventually found protection by creating trade unions, but this was also the end of the struggle against wage labour, for it 'marked an acceptance of the permanence of wage labour' and of capitalism. This also meant accepting reform rather than revolution. He believes that the law is no longer as 'blatantly and unashamedly class-slanted' as it was in the 17th century: 'Democratisation has made the law seem less alien' and 'the ideal of a law which represents the wishes of the community has changed attitudes'. 'When we don't like laws today we organise to try to get them changed.'

Who but Christopher Hill would delight at least this reader by concluding a major study of 17th century English history with the following paragraph:

The law, like the doors of the Ritz Hotel, has long been open to rich and poor alike: only the poor don't often think of mentioning it publicly because the Ritz Hotel is beyond their reach. Today we glamorise train-robbers rather than pirates. As I write these words London traffic is blocked by crowds observing the semi-state funeral of the gangster Ronnie Kray. Always the streets of our cities are lined with homeless people sleeping rough; but no less a person than our Prime Minister reassures us that there is no justification for anyone to offend the delicate sensibilities of well-housed, well-paid and well-fed citizens by indulging in begging. Beggars may even discourage foreign tourists from visiting London, he moans. In the national interest they must disappear—to somewhere where they will not be visible. Some may see evidence of progress in the fact that we no longer flog the impotent poor out of town.

From the kingdom of necessity to the kingdom of freedom: Morris's *News From Nowhere*

PAUL O'FLINN

Nineteen ninety six is the year the liberal middle classes finally went off William Morris. They may have been happy enough to have his fabrics in their living rooms but this year, prompted by the commemorations surrounding the centenary of his death, they have had a closer look at the man and his politics. They don't like what they see. 'He was not just a wallpaper designer, but a revolutionary socialist—a combination that might have been the invention of a satirist,' sneered Deyan Sudjic in the *Guardian*.[1] In a word, keep the wallpaper but for God's sake skip the socialism, a position pioneered by the Labour Party some time ago. Tim Hilton issued a stern warning to readers of the *Independent on Sunday* that 'his politics are not only irrelevant but objectionable'.[2] Deyan Sudjic spelt out that warning: 'Morris can be seen as an inspiration...for the Khmer Rouge... He was no totalitarian, but in the Phnom Penh of Year Zero, there is a hideous echo of *News From Nowhere*.' The least I can do for Morris in his centenary year is to dispose of this sort of contemptuous incomprehension and try to tell the truth about *News From Nowhere*. I am going to focus on just that one text and its context. My account, therefore, fits inside the longer view of Morris's whole life and work offered by Hassan Mahamdallie in the previous issue of this journal.

Morris and the anarchists

The obvious place to start looking for that truth is the novel's opening paragraphs and it also happens to be the best place to understand the point and the politics of Morris's text. An unnamed narrator describes a brisk discussion about 'what would happen on the Morrow of the Revolution' at a meeting of the executive committee of Morris's party, the Socialist League:

> *There were six persons present, and consequently six sections of the party were represented, four of which had strong but divergent anarchist opinions. One of the sections, says our friend, a man whom he knows very well indeed, sat almost silent at the beginning of the discussion, but at last got drawn into it, and finished by roaring out very loud, and damning all the rest for fools.*

'One of the sections' is in effect Morris himself, who on his way home after the meeting:

> *...found himself musing on the subject-matter of discussion, but still discontentedly and unhappily. 'If I could but see a day of it,' he said to himself; 'if I could but see it!'* [3]

The novel that follows is just that—an attempt to 'see a day of it' and describe life in a comfortably post-revolutionary society. Because most of us nowadays read the novel in a modern edition, such as the Penguin I am quoting from, it is easy to lose sight of the explosive nature of this beginning. *News From Nowhere* first appeared, not in a floppy paperback with an inoffensive picture on the front cover, but serialised in *Commonweal*. *Commonweal*, as the subtitle on the front page insisted, was 'The Official Journal of the Socialist League'; it was the League's eight page weekly paper and Morris was its editor. When he had taken on that post with Edward Aveling as his co-editor, they had accepted that they were 'acting as delegates of the Socialist League, and under its direct control'. This was publically stated on the first page of the (then monthly) first edition back in February 1885.

In that context, the opening paragraphs of *News From Nowhere* read very differently. Morris ran them on the front page of *Commonweal* on 11 January 1890 as a blast, a prolonged 'roaring out very loud' at the 'fools' with their 'strong but divergent anarchist opinions' who by that date controlled the party, the paper and its editor, William Morris. True, each week the paper ran a formal disclaimer on its centre page to the effect that:

> *The **Commonweal** is the official organ of the Socialist League; but unless definitely so announced by the editors, no article is to be taken as expressing*

in more than a general way the views of the League as a body.[4]

But these opening paragraphs of *News From Nowhere* are not even in 'a general way the views of the League as a body' but rather a furious challenge to that body and the shambles it was becoming. It was a challenge that got Morris the sack as editor within four months and before his serial was half finished, although such was his drawing power for the paper that the serial ran through to its conclusion on 4 October 1890.

What I want to argue, then, is that *News From Nowhere* is best understood as Morris's impassioned argument with the political direction being taken by his party. It was an argument conducted in the party's paper and through his novel which that paper serialised. On the one hand, for five years he had expressed his socialism through his commitment to the Socialist League, worked for them, learnt from them. On the other, he was now taking on the anarchists who dominated its executive. It was out of that dialectical tension, at once blindly infuriating and yet massively stimulating, that *News From Nowhere* was made and shaped.

The story of the anarchist takeover of the Socialist League has been told often enough.[5] Briefly, the Socialist League's insistence on a revolutionary rather than a parliamentary road to socialism came to a head at the party's Third Annual Conference on 29 May 1887. That position, part of its original 1884 constitution, was challenged by a motion from the Croydon branch which demanded: 'Its [the Socialist League's] objects shall be sought to be obtained by every available means, parliamentary or otherwise.' The motion was withdrawn and the attempt to change the party's direction failed again at the Fourth Annual Conference in 1888. In the wake of those decisions, many of the party's leading members—Eleanor Marx, Edward Aveling, Belfort Bax— drifted away.

Morris supported the constitution that he had helped to write, yet he fought hard but unsuccessfully to avoid a split. On 23 February 1887, before the Third Conference, he had noted in his diary: 'I may as well state here that my intention is if possible to prevent the quarrel coming to a head between the two sections—parliamentary and anti-parliamentary—and which are pretty much commensurate with the collectivists and anarchists.' As the split became inevitable, he noted glumly in the same diary a few weeks later on 30 March: 'Whatever happens, I fear however that as an organisation we shall come to nothing'.[6]

News From Nowhere ran as a weekly serial in *Commonweal* from 11 January 1890 to 4 October 1890. It runs across that split as it worked its way through the party and its paper and hence the novel inevitably becomes a part of that ragged, rending process, at times contesting the split, at times contributing to it, but always driving towards Morris's vision of revolutionary socialism and the steps needed to achieve it. I would like to look first at these political struggles as they raged unevenly around the novel and then move on to examine the way they help to structure the text itself.

It was in the last quarter of the 19th century that anarchism had its most profound impact on British political life. Because it centres on the needs and desires of individuals, anarchism is instinctively hostile to any form of centralised authority. This in turn tends to condemn it to a flashy, fragmented and impotent existence on the margins of political life, a wonderful source of libertarian slogans yet hopeless as a focus for effective joint action. But it was precisely that impotence that an international conference of anarchist groups, the International Revolutionary Congress held in London in July 1881, sought to overcome. The conference was impatient with the inevitably slow, tedious and often apparently fruitless work of socialist education. It cut short that dull plod with a slogan—'Propaganda by deed'. Propaganda by deed aimed to galvanise and inspire oppressed masses wearied by radical rhetoric that left the world unchanged and the rich unmoved. The slogan certainly inspired a series of bombings and assassinations across European cities for the rest of the century which certainly changed the world and moved the rich—but in wholly reactionary ways. For now all that lay in the future. In 1881 one of the participants at Congress, where the new slogan, Propaganda by deed, was adopted, was a young man called Frank Kitz. In 1885 Kitz joined the Socialist League and it was Kitz who, with David Nicoll, took over as joint editor of *Commonweal* when Morris was removed in May 1890.[7]

As those who had attempted to shift the Socialist League towards parliamentary politics drifted away in the wake of their defeats at the 1887 and 1888 party conferences, Morris realised that the remaining revolutionary socialists like himself would have to confront anarchist politics if the Socialist League was not to end up as a straightforwardly anarchist party. He said as much to fellow party member Bruce Glasier in the wake of the decisions at the 1888 conference:

> *We have got rid of the parliamentarians, and now our anarchist friends will want to drive the team. However, we have the Council and the **Commonweal** safe with us for at least a twelve month, and that is something to be thankful for.*[8]

He set about thwarting their attempt to drive the team with a letter that he wrote to *Commonweal* and printed on 18 May 1889. It started with a deliberately unsettling insistence: 'I call myself a communist and have no wish to qualify that word by joining any other to it.' That implicit attack on anarchism became explicit as the letter proceeded:

> *If freedom from authority means the assertion of the advisability or possibility of an individual man doing what he pleases always and under all circumstances, this is an absolute negation of society, and makes communism as the highest expression of society impossible; and when you begin to qualify this assertion of the right to do as you please by adding 'as long as you don't interfere with other people's rights to do the same', the exercise of some kind of authority becomes necessary.*

The language here is calculatedly extreme—'doing what he pleases always and under all circumstances...an absolute negation of society... makes communism...impossible'. Morris is plainly trying to provoke a fight with the anarchists in and around the party, and he soon had several takers. All tried to respond to the question of authority and how it should be exercised in a pre-revolutionary party and a post-revolutionary society. J Armsden, writing to *Commonweal* on 1 June 1889, flatly denied 'any necessity for authority', a denial repeated by an anarchist, who wrote on 22 June: 'I should deny the necessity for the exercise of authority...free association is the only guarantee of the due observance of our equal liberty.' The same issue of *Commonweal* included a letter from H Davis, elected that same month to the Council of the Socialist League at its Fifth Annual Conference. Davis picked up Morris's opening challenge ('I call myself a communist and have no wish to qualify that word by joining any other to it') and responded directly: 'I, on the other hand, call myself an anarchist-communist, and have no wish to separate the two words.' Morris's challenge on the question of authority was not answered with careful consideration and substantiated rebuttal. Davis simply swept past it on the momentum of rhetorical assertions: 'I will admit of no compulsion of man over man... The anarchist seek [sic] freedom through individual liberty by affirming the sovereignty of the individual.'

What we have here is a small part of the debate between revolutionary socialists and anarchists that sounded across the paper in the following months. The notices that the paper carried every week on its back page are particularly revealing. Frequently a column listing a series of books and pamphlets by Morris for sale stood side by side with an advertisement for *Freiheit*, 'International Organ of the German-speaking Anarchists', available from the *Commonweal* office, or for *La Revolte*, 'Organe Communiste-Anarchiste'.[9] On 7 June 1890, after Morris had lost the editorship but while he was still writing for the paper, *Commonweal* ran a note welcoming the appearance of a new paper, *The Anarchist Labour Leaf*, launched by the East London Communist-

Anarchist Group. In one of those small but significant flickers familiar then and since to close readers of the left press, the paper's weekly round up of strike news, always headlined 'The Labour Struggle', was retitled on 19 July 1890 'The Labour Revolt'.

As factions battled for control of the paper, the erratic swings of David Nicoll, one of its most frequent contributors, seem to me to be particularly revealing. Described by Thompson as 'a highly-strung and unstable intellectual',[10] he and Frank Kitz took over from Morris as editors of *Commonweal* at the end of May 1890. By 6 September, with the *News From Nowhere* serial still running, he appeared to be pushing the paper in uninhibitedly anarchist directions. That week he led with his own article, 'Why we Do Not Believe in Parliamentary Action' and followed it directly with Part 3 of 'Revolutionary Government' by the most famous anarchist of the lot, Peter Kropotkin. Yet the following week, in the 13 September edition, Nicoll published a letter from himself, challenging Kropotkin's assumptions and asking a series of basic questions. 'What will the anarchists do', he demanded, if after a successful revolution, 'provisions run short? Who is to direct the men...to get the supplies of food?' Two weeks later, on 27 September, Nicoll went after the anarchists again in a piece entitled 'An Anarchist Paper on the Socialist Movement', defending the role of revolutionary socialists in the dock strike against criticism in the anarchist paper *La Revolte*. Yet Nicoll it was who eventually and effectively sank the paper in April 1892 when he ran an article titled 'Are These Men Fit to Live?' This was directed at the judges responsible for sentencing a group of anarchists to ten years penal servitude for planning bombings. The article did no discernible damage to the judges but quickly earned Nicoll a 16 month sentence for incitement to murder.[11]

Before things fell apart to that extent, Morris had tried to hold the centre of the party together. Even after his removal from the editorship of *Commonweal* in May 1890, he was prepared to argue for his own and his party's politics in the paper. The very next week, in an article headed 'Anti-Parliamentary', he explained and defended the Socialist League's position on abstention from parliamentary elections. The aim of parliament, he insisted, is 'the upholding of privilege; the society of rich and poor'; it was therefore 'a hopeless enterprise' to try to 'jockey parliament into socialism' . He concluded by recommending socialists to direct their energy to 'strengthen your own organisations'.[12]

A road to socialism that is neither parliamentary nor anarchist may be familiar enough to readers of this journal, but it was not one that was readily available in the 19th century. Morris wore himself out helping to lay its foundations.

News From Nowhere and Commonweal

In the light of these facts about *Commonweal*, its politics and its struggles, I think we can begin to make much clearer sense of *News From Nowhere*, its strengths and its silences. An enormous source of power that flowed very directly from the novel's serialisation in the paper is surely that Morris was able to write a novel without compromises. *News From Nowhere* is a book that talks directly about socialism and about how to achieve it, which is what readers of *Commonweal* wanted to know about. Its pages are not clogged with the sugary pap demanded by middle class publishers devising inoffensive leisure products for alienated readers. Morris was thus able to write what one critic has called an anti-novel,[13] as he himself makes clear through one of his characters, Ellen. She looks back dismissively on the claims of 19th century realist fiction:

> *As for your books, they were well enough for times when intelligent people had but little else in which they could take pleasure, and when their needs must supplement the sordid miseries of their own lives with imaginations of the lives of other people. But I say flatly that in spite of all their cleverness and vigour, and capacity for story telling, there is something loathsome about them. Some of them, indeed, do here and there show some feeling for those whom the history-books call 'poor', and of the misery of whose lives we have some inkling; but presently they give it up, and towards the end of the story we must be contented to see the hero and heroine living happily in an island of bliss on other people's troubles; and that after a long series of sham troubles (or mostly sham) of their own making, illustrated by dreary intro-spective nonsense about their feelings and aspirations, and all the rest of it; while the world must even then have gone on its way, and dug and sewed and baked and built and carpentered round these useless animals.*[14]

As that long last sentence unfolds, Morris veers from irritated splutter ('all the rest of it') to calculated offence to the tastes and expectations of standard novel readers ('dreary introspective nonsense about...feel-ings'). The people who paid a penny for *Commonweal* at street corner meetings, at demonstrations and on picket lines were looking for a story that spoke directly to their anger, desires and hopes, that spoke about how one day people would fight for and win a better world for them-selves and their children. *News From Nowhere* was written for those people. It was not written for standard issue 19th century novel readers anxious for tales of moral crises over breaches of good manners or minute fluctuations in the finely tuned, narrowly directed sensibilities of the upper middle classes and those frantic to join them. And it was certainly not written for 20th century *Guardian* journalists.

And another thing—publication in *Commonweal* allowed Morris to focus his story sharply, secure in the knowledge that issues inevitably marginalised by that sharp focus were clarified by their coverage elsewhere in the paper. Thus, for example, one of the great strengths of *Commonweal* was its resolute internationalism. The Socialist League's 'Statement of Principles', which ran on the back page of the paper nearly every week, insisted:

> *This revolutionary socialism must be international. The change which would put an end to the struggle between man and man, would destroy it also between nation and nation. One harmonious system of federation throughout the whole of civilisation would take the place of the old destructive rivalries. There would be no great centres breeding race hatred and commercial jealousy.*[15]

That internationalist commitment informed the paper. Every week the centre page carried a list of publications received; on 21 June 1890, for example, 51 journals are listed from, amongst others, Italy, the US, Sweden, Cuba, Germany and Argentina. Those papers provided the basis for an 'International News' column that was a regular feature and carried items from places as far apart as Australia, Denmark, Russia and Southern Africa. In the spring of 1890, while *News From Nowhere* was running at the front of the paper, the middle pages carried regular reports from Morris's daughter May on the strike fund set up by the Socialist League to assist French blanket weavers in Cours.[16]

In that context it is therefore quite wrong to criticise Morris as some have done[17] for confining his text to England and failing to address the issue of world revolution. *News From Nowhere* is about the local unfolding of a struggle that was comprehensively dealt with in the rest of the paper. Morris used his serial to work out in detail what socialism might mean for Clara, Dick and Ellen in London while other pages in *Commonweal* complemented that with news of the struggle for socialism in New York, Melbourne and Havana.

And that wasn't all. The class struggle politics of the Socialist League and its paper gave Morris the support and the context to develop his vision of socialism in *News From Nowhere* in ways quite impossible in a novel prepared for conventional publishing by a conventional publisher. In particular, it encouraged him to expand his attack on those dilute notions of socialism then associated with Fabianism which in turn were to become central to the thinking of the Labour Party as it took root in the next decade. A fortnight after *News From Nowhere* started running in *Commonweal*, Morris contributed to the paper a long review of *Fabian Essays in Socialism*. His review of a volume which, as he noted, included designs by his daughter May, was conducted with his habitual kindliness; it could be obtained post free from *Commonweal* offices and,

'I assume that all socialists will read it.' However, the review is also
marked by his habitual honesty; the Fabian 'theory of tactics'—in
essence, the 'rollicking opportunism' of Sidney Webb—is a 'disastrous
move.' At its core is 'the parliamentary struggle which we do not believe
in'.[18] From there it is only a short step to *News From Nowhere*'s famous
vision of the Houses of Parliament in the future being used as a storage
place for manure.[19] But, more extensively, his critique of Fabianism in
this 25 January review provides the basis for the novel's longest chapter,
Chapter XVII, which appeared four months later. It ran for five numbers
of *Commonweal* from 17 May to 14 June and described in careful detail
the process of arriving at socialism not through parliament but as the
result of a raggedly escalating process of unemployment, demonstrations, ruling class reaction, general strike and civil war.

In short, Morris centres on what *Commonweal* was focused on. As
well as special articles on particular strikes, it ran a weekly column
headed 'The Labour Struggle', a roundup of news covering every major
and minor dispute. Morris chimed in with this coverage, for example
with an article on 22 March 1890 headed 'The Great Coal Strike', that
insisted, 'It is a battle, not a mere business dispute.' Or again six weeks
later on 3 May, in a front page piece headed 'Labour Day', he noted a
'growing comprehension of socialism…underlying all the strikes which
have lately taken place, and which has been quite different to that of the
strikes of the decade before the revival of socialism in this country.' In
tandem with *Commonweal*, Morris worked out week by week a theory of
the transition to socialism based on the industrial struggles of the late
19th century and one of the functions of *News From Nowhere* was to see
that transition enacted in the 20th century.[20]

But inevitably, as he wrote his way towards a vision of socialism in
News From Nowhere through the medium of *Commonweal*, he also
shared some of the limitations of the Socialist League and its paper. For
all the sane, brave things about sexuality and its expression in Chapter
IX, 'Concerning Love', most modern readers find the book's views on
gender and on women's roles uselessly dated.[21] Jan Marsh in particular
has written sharply but sympathetically on that subject and I don't need
to add to what she has to say here.[22]

From the 'Manifesto of the Socialist League' that Morris helped to
draft and that was carried on the front page of the first edition of
Commonweal in February 1885, to the 'Statement of Principles' that ran
on the back page every week, the Socialist League offered a relentless
and welcome insistence on class and class issues whose downside was
that its rare pronouncements on sexual politics were depressingly conventional. That conventionality pervades *News From Nowhere* and is
only partly redeemed by characters like Ellen, who seems to spring from

sectors of Morris's imagination that escaped political conditioning. The other exception, Philippa the headstone carver who appears briefly in Chapter XXVI is, significantly enough, an afterthought, not part of the original serial and only added when it was revised to become a book.

But it is around the issue of anarchism, as I have already suggested, that *News From Nowhere* offers the most consistent challenge to the way the Socialist League was developing. The novel describes in detail the process by which a class rides the uneven momentum of history as it is in part carried and in part struggles together towards power with no assistance anywhere from heroic bomb throwers and their 'propaganda by deed'. Once in power, Chapter XIV explains how democratic control is exercised in a small socialist community. The anarchist alternative, 'to wit, that every man should be quite independent of every other, and that thus the tyranny of society should be abolished', is simply dismissed by the narrator and one of the protagonists as they 'burst out laughing very heartily' at the mere idea.[23]

From the kingdom of necessity to the kingdom of freedom

I have tried to argue that *News From Nowhere* is a dialectical novel, a text produced by the creative tensions between Morris, the Socialist League which he was on the point of leaving, and *Commonweal*, the paper which serialised his story but whose editorship he lost while the serial was still running. To some extent those tensions obviously drove Morris to set the novel far in the future, well away from the sectarian strife of the present, as he himself makes clear in the opening paragraphs. Yet he is also doing much more than that. In 1892, two years after the serialisation of *News From Nowhere*, Edward Aveling, formerly co-editor of *Commonweal* with Morris, published the first English translation of what was to become a classic Marxist text, Engels' *Socialism, Utopian and Scientific* (originally published in French in 1880). Engels himself was a regular contributor to *Commonweal*; in *Socialism, Utopian and Scientific* he writes of humanity's ascent from prehistory, the present, into the beginnings of real human history, the communist future:

> *Man's own social organisation, hitherto confronting him as a necessity imposed by nature and history, now becomes the result of his own free action. The extraneous objective forces that have hitherto governed history pass under the control of man himself. Only from that time will man himself, more and more consciously, make his own history—only from that time will the social causes set in movement by him have…the results intended by him. It is the ascent of man from the kingdom of necessity to the kingdom of freedom.*[24]

That is surely the context in which to read *News From Nowhere*, as the first fully human novel, a first story about people as they can and will be, liberated from all the alienation, reification, exploitation and complex varieties of crap that fill the pages of 19th century fiction, the fiction of prehistory. That is the way to read Morris's novel, a pioneering attempt to imagine the lives of the first free human beings, rather than to go searching as some have done for comically irrelevant parallels with *The Wind in the Willows* or Walter Scott.[25]

And seeing it in that way helps us to avoid another fallacy about Morris. This, with a sad shake of the head, insists that because of his revolutionary purism he failed to attach himself to the way the world in general and British socialism in particular was going.[26] Within a decade there were Labour MPs and within a generation there was a Labour government. Morris's utterly intransigent version of revolutionary Marxism has meant that he and his novel have always been marginal to those developments. Simply, he got it wrong; there was no successful socialist revolution in 1952, as *News From Nowhere* claims.

As I started writing this, Tony Blair was in New York, reassuring Wall Street bankers that the next Labour government would make no difference to them and their investments and their profits. In terms of electoral politics, that was of course an entirely sensible thing to do. If the next Labour government is not to be promptly derailed the way previous ones have been by the movements of global capital, then the more reassurances Tony Blair can give to Wall Street the better. But it surely also proves that, even if Morris got it wrong in the short run, he was right in the long run and there really is no parliamentary road to Clause Four, never mind to socialism.

Of course, the easy cynical answer to that is to say that in the long run we're all dead. Well, yes and no. You're dead, I'm dead, but humanity isn't dead; the dream of human liberation doesn't die. And the longer we go on without reaching that dream, the more important it becomes to get it right whenever the chance to realise it presents itself. We don't have many better maps for finding that dream than *News From Nowhere*.

Notes

1   *The Guardian*, 3 May 1996, p 6.
2   *Independent on Sunday*, magazine section, 5 May 1996, p21.
3   C Wilmer (ed), *William Morris: News from Nowhere and other Writings* (Harmondsworth, 1993), pp43-44. I have used this edition throughout simply because it is the most readily available. However, like all 20th century editions of *News From Nowhere*, it is based on the revised edition of the novel that Morris prepared for its first appearance as a book, published in Boston in 1890 and in London in 1891 by Reeves & Turner. There are important differences between these two editions which have been detailed by A MacDonald, 'The Revision of *News From Nowhere*', *Journal of the William Morris Society*, 3:2, Summer 1976.

But these differences do not affect my argument and I have therefore used the Penguin edition because it is the most convenient for readers.

4   See, for example, that same edition of *Commonweal*, 11 January 1890, p12.

5   The rest of this paragraph is based on those accounts I have found most useful: Y Kapp, *Eleanor Marx: The Crowded Years 1884-1898* (London, 1976), E P Thompson, *William Morris: Romantic to Revolutionary* (London, 1977), and the Introduction to N Salmon (ed), *William Morris: Political Writings—Contributions to **Justice** and **Commonweal** 1883-1890* (Bristol, 1994).

6   F Boos (ed), *William Morris's Socialist Diary* (London, 1985), pp37 and 46.

7   Details here from H Oliver, *The International Anarchist Movement in Late Victorian London* (London, 1983). My thanks to David Nash for drawing my attention to this book, a mine of information on its subject.

8   E P Thompson, op cit, p509.

9   See, for example, *Commonweal*, 8 March 1890, p80; 22 March 1890, p96; and 5 April 1890, p112.

10 E P Thompson, op cit, p508.

11 For details, see H Oliver, op cit, ch 4.

12 *Commonweal*, 7 June 1890, pp180-181.

13 See P Brantlinger, '*News from Nowhere*: Morris's Socialist Anti-Novel', *Victorian Studies*, XIX, September 1975.

14 *News From Nowhere*, op cit, pp175-176.

15 This is taken from the 'Statement of Principles' on the back page of *Commonweal*, 15 March 1890. Very occasionally pressure on space seems to have led to its disappearance in a given week—see, for example, 5 July and 27 September 1890.

16 See, for example, *Commonweal*, 22 March and 10 May 1890.

17 See, for example, J Crump, 'How the Change Came: *News from Nowhere* and Revolution', in S Coleman and P O'Sullivan (eds), *William Morris and **News from Nowhere**: A Vision for Our Time* (Bideford, 1990).

18 *Commonweal*, 25 January 1890, p28.

19 *News From Nowhere*, p69.

20 I am aware that most historians regard the Socialist League, like the Social Democratic Federation, as disastrously underestimating the political importance of New Unionism and the rise in strike action of the late 19th century—see, for example, H Collins, 'The Marxism of the Social Democratic Federation', in A Briggs and J Saville (eds), *Essays in Labour History 1886-1923* (London, 1971). This may have been true in practice but is certainly not borne out by my reading of *Commonweal*. Engels noted this contradiction between theory and practice when he complained in a letter to Sorge dated 19 April 1890 about the Socialist League's penchant for 'making phrases and otherwise doing nothing'.

21 A significant recent exception is F MacCarthy, *William Morris: A Life for Our Time* (London, 1994). She finds *Nowhere* 'a place of real sexual equality' (p588). She also persistently misnames one of the novel's main characters, Dick, as Robert and probably needs to read the book again.

22 See her *Jane and May Morris: A Biographical Story* (London, 1986), and in particular her piece in Coleman and O'Sullivan, op cit.

23 *News From Nowhere*, p120.

24 F Engels, *Socialism, Utopian and Scientific,* in *Marx, Engels, Lenin, Four Classic Texts on the Principles of Socialism* (London, 1960), p144. This seems to me a simpler and more accurate way of describing the relationship between Engels' text and Morris's than the rather tangled argument about the two books that Thompson conducts with Abensour in E P Thompson, op cit, pp787-791.

25 See, respectively, Wilmer, pxxxvi, and J Redmond (ed), *William Morris: **News from Nowhere*** (London, 1970), pxiii.

26 See for example E P Thompson, op cit, Part III, Chs 5 and 6 in particular.

Bookwatch: Palestine and the Middle East 'peace process'

CLARE FERMONT

When Yasser Arafat shook hands with Israeli president Yitzhak Rabin on the White House lawn in September 1993, he was not beginning a 'peace process', he was surrendering the Palestinian struggle. The deal he had just signed—the Oslo accords—abandoned self-determination for Palestinians and therefore abandoned millions of Palestinian refugees. The state of Israel had won international recognition and legitimacy. It was also accepted by most Arab leaders, giving Israel free access to Arab markets, without Israel even conceding sovereignty over the Arab land captured in 1967, let alone 1948. The Israeli authorities had not forfeited much in the scraps of land in the West Bank and Gaza now administered by the Palestine National Authority. The government in Tel Aviv kept control of the key issues: land, water, security, foreign policy—even the air.

This was the sum reward for decades of sacrifice and resistance by Palestinians. No other liberation movement this century has settled for so little. Precisely because the deal offers so little to the overwhelming majority of Palestinians, it cannot put a stop to Palestinian resistance and will certainly not herald a new age of peace in the region. If anything, there will be more violence and repression.

The history of the Palestinians has been covered by a vast amount of literature. Much of it supports Zionist myths, demonises the Arabs and conceals the role of imperialism. A good place to start, therefore, is with three books which give a general history without reproducing these distortions.

Our Roots Are Still Alive has the feel of a school text book, but is in fact a powerful socialist history of the Palestinians from the 19th century to the mid-1970s.[1] Although sometimes simplistic, it is packed with wonderful quotations and crucial facts which expose Zionism and provoke fury on behalf of its victims. The book shows that from the 1920s the Palestinians have been fighting against mighty powers which have sought to dominate their country and undermine their struggles. British and Zionist colonisation culminating in 1948 with the establishment of the state of Israel involved a level of terror horrific enough to drive nearly a million Palestinian Arabs from their homes. Since then, the Palestinians have been hounded by a state armed to the teeth and backed wholeheartedly by American imperialism. *Our Roots Are Still Alive* also highlights that throughout this century, Arab leaders have used and abused the Palestinian struggle to protect their own interests.

The Gun and the Olive Branch, by *The Guardian* journalist David Hirst, is an uncompromisingly anti-Zionist, pro-Palestinian account of the same period with the added advantage that it is beautifully written.[2] For a more political and polemical attack on the myths, there is no better book than Noam Chomsky's *The Fateful Triangle*.[3] This is especially strong on exposing the role of US imperialism and debunking Zionist propaganda. For example, Chomsky discloses that in 1982, 'The total number of Israelis killed in all acts of terror from 1967 is 282, less than the number killed by Israel's air terrorists in Beirut on July 17-18 1981 in "retaliation" after a PLO response to Israeli bombing that broke the cease-fire'.[4] John Rose's excellent pamphlet *Israel: The Hijack State* is an accessible account of the role of imperialism and Zionism and is an excellent starting point for anyone unfamilier with the issues.[5]

Another book worth looking at, mainly because of its amazing photographs, is *The Palestinians*.[6] A simple and moving text by Jonathan Dimbleby (written in his more radical days) is brought dramatically to life by the brilliant photographer Donald McCullin. In this book the old cliche is true—the pictures do say more than the words, and they leave little doubt about the extent of Israeli repression and Palestinian suffering.

If these books are difficult to find, Edward Said's books offer well written, accurate accounts of recent Palestinian history.[7] So too does *The Palestinians: The Road to Nationhood*, by David McDowall, which covers the entire century up to and beyond the Oslo accords.[8]

This *Bookwatch* focuses on books that offer greater insight into the politics of the Palestinian resistance, especially at the high points of the struggle, as these help us to understand why Arafat accepted so little.

Before 1948

The best starting point is *Zionism: False Messiah* by Nathan Weinstock.[9] Although marred by the author's attempts to prove an orthodox Trotskyist position at every turn, the book provides an excellent summary of how the Zionist movement was dependent upon and received the backing of British imperialism, and how it sought to settle and colonise Palestine.[10]

The Zionist colonial project was based on excluding rather than directly exploiting the Palestinian Arabs, on buying up their land and establishing a separate economy. This policy affected both the Jewish left and the Arab nationalist movement. Simha Flapan, a left wing Zionist, gives us a good account of how the Zionist movement interacted with the Arabs up to 1948. In *Zionism and the Palestinians* he spells out how the settlers were increasingly driven by the extreme right wing Zionists, in particular by the founder of the Revisionist movement, Wladimir (Zev) Jabotinsky, himself influenced by Mussolini's black-shirts.[11] Weinstock shows that even socialist ideology among the Jewish pioneers was heavily tinged with colonialism and that Zionism blunted class consciousness and prevented unity between Arabs and Jews.[12]

The Zionist agenda crystallised Arab nationalism in Palestine, a movement that was already growing in the region in response to Western imperialism. Weinstock shows how the movement in Palestine was led by reactionary, backward, semi-feudal landlords. The influx of Jewish capital and the exclusion of Arabs from the developing part of the economy resulted in an underdeveloped Arab bourgeoisie and working class. More detail about the class nature of the Palestinian movement is provided in the excellent *Palestine and the Palestinians* by Pamela Ann Smith (see below).[13]

Arab strikes and protests against Jewish settlements and British colonial rule intensified as waves of Jewish immigrants, fleeing horrific persecution in Europe, poured into Palestine in 1934 and 1935. The resentment exploded in 1936 with a six month general strike. This began the 'Palestinian Revolt' which lasted for three years.

The best book on the revolt, by the wonderful Palestinian novelist and painter Ghassan Kanafani, is sadly out of print.[14] In a thrilling account, he brings to life the mobilisation of virtually all Palestinians. He also describes graphically the brutality of British troops, who used techniques such as collective punishments and the destruction of whole villages that the Israeli state would later copy. The scale of the repression eventually crushed the revolt in 1939, paving the way for the Zionist victory in 1948.

Letters from Palestine by Thomas Hodgkin, a British bureaucrat in the Palestine administration, is also a fascinating account of the revolt at its height, as well as its decay as the leadership misdirected it.[15] He explains how the strike was undermined by the Arab High Committee, the co-ordinating body of the movement that was dominated by landlords who gradually drifted towards fascism.

The activities of the Jewish and Arab left in this period are covered in detail by Weinstock. The sole organisation that had a formally internationalist position, the Palestine Communist Party (PCP), is also analysed by Musa Budeiri in *The Palestine Communist Party*.[16] He shows how the party line zig-zagged according to the whims of Moscow.[17] Again and again the party took up a disastrous stance towards the nationalist movement, and eventually split along Jewish/Arab lines. Attempts at unity between the Arab and Jewish left in the 1940s and 1950s are also covered by Joel Beinin in *Was the Red Flag Flying There?*[18] Despite glamorising some of these attempts, Beinin does reveal how the Jewish left was unable to distance itself from Zionism. He also shows that the failures of the PCP meant that after 1948 there was no genuinely international socialist alternative to either Zionism or Arab nationalism.

Several books demonstrate Britain's role in supporting the formation of a Jewish homeland in Palestine. A fascinating inside view is provided in *Orientations* by Sir Ronald Storrs, the British governor general of mandate Palestine.[19] He provides a detailed account of British/Zionist/Palestinian relations in the 1920s and the dealings of the Foreign Office with the Jewish Agency and their favoured Arab leader, Haj Amin el-Husseini, the mufti of Jerusalem. He explains how and why the British ruling class chose Zionism, rather than Arab nationalism, to maintain their influence in Palestine. From his pen comes the famous quote that a Jewish state in Palestine would provide 'for England "a little loyal Jewish Ulster" in a sea of potentially hostile Arabism'.[20]

The PLO

It took a generation for Palestinians to recover from the catastrophe of 1948. One reason for this was the sheer scale of the defeat. The other was the reliance on the new breed of Arab nationalist leaders, spearheaded by the Egyptian leader, Gamal Abdul Nasser. The story of the Palestinians' recovery is told by Rosemary Sayigh in *Palestinians: From Peasants to Revolutionaries*.[21] Written in the late 1970s, it is a classic history from below, although tinted—and tainted—by her emotional attachment to guerrilla warfare. She describes through the mouths of Palestinians their dislocation after 1948, and the discrimination and marginalisation they experienced in the refugee camps. Focusing on Lebanon, she dramatically recounts the transformation of peasants into a movement of mass resistance. Utterly readable, Sayigh's book reveals the tenacity of spirit among Palestinians that has survived seemingly endless disasters.

Two other books offer good general introductions to the development and politics of the PLO and Fatah, the main organisation within the PLO. *The Politics of Palestinian Nationalism*, written in the early 1970s, was one of the first Western accounts to tackle the subject in an unbiased way.[22] It shows, among other things, how Palestinian nationalism developed in the wake of the humiliation of Arab nationalism and Nasser in the 1967 Arab-Israeli war. *The Palestinian Liberation Organisation* by Helena Cobban is a committed and comprehensive academic work, though the political analysis is somewhat superficial.[23] She demonstrates that, whatever the faults of the armed struggle, the Palestinian resistance in the 1960s and 1970s re-established the Palestinian identity, both among Palestinians and internationally. She reminds us that their struggle took place against the background of an attitude summed up by Israeli premier Golda Meir's famous words of 1969: 'It was not as though there was a Palestinian people...and we came and threw them out and took their country away from them. They did not exist.'[24]

These authors and others[25] show that although the new Israeli state had expelled Palestinians indiscriminately, regardless of their class, the fate of the refugees varied considerably according to their wealth and education. Many of the former Palestinian bourgeoisie ended up in the Gulf states, and it was from their ranks that the PLO was organised, leading eventually to the ousting of the old 'aristocratic' leadership.

Pamela Ann Smith offers one of the best class analyses of this period.[26] She describes how the Palestinian diaspora was influenced by the oil economy in the Gulf and how Fatah was a product of this. Yasser Arafat, for example, who became the leader of Fatah, was well on his way to becoming a millionaire in Kuwait. Smith provides a fascinating account of how the Palestinian bourgeoisie made their money and were fully integrated with Arab capitalism. They lacked a state, so they created the basis of a Palestinian state in exile.

Fatah stressed that all Palestinians should unite, regardless of class, in 'mass revolutionary violence' against their common and sole enemy, Israel. No other battle should or would be fought. Such politics are brought to life in the many biographies of Yasser Arafat. The best of these, despite the sycophancy, is *Arafat: Terrorist or Peacemaker?* by Alan Hart, written in collaboration with the PLO leadership, including Arafat himself.[27] In the early days, as students in Cairo in the 1950s, Arafat and his colleagues believed the armed struggle would provoke a crisis where Egypt and other Arab countries would be forced to engage Israel in war. When the 1967 war came and went in defeat, guerrilla tactics were sustained in order to cement the Palestinian identity and to maintain pressure on Israel and Arab rulers. Fatah's leaders always recognised that a military victory over Israel was impossible.

Hart's book reveals the extraordinary courage of Fatah activists, including its leaders, and the tremendous sacrifices they all made. It also reveals the heart of the PLO's political weakness—the continuing reliance on Arab rulers and the policy of 'non-interference' in countries hosting Palestinian refugees. He writes about an event in 1969:

> *Against all expectations, he* [Khalad Hassan, a PLO leader] *had persuaded King Feisal of Saudi Arabia to support Fatah... As time proved, with Saudi Arabia on its side Fatah was indestructible—as long as it was pursuing policies the Saudis would endorse.*

Similar insights can be gained from the autobiography of Salah Khalaf, better known as Abu Iyad, one of the founding members of Fatah.[28] It shows how the lifestyles of the PLO leaders increasingly distanced them from most Palestinians, often leaving them unaware of the real aspirations of the millions of refugees they purported to represent.[29]

The story of the Palestinian left, which grew in the early 1960s in opposition to the leadership of Fatah, is covered in several of these books, particularly those by Cobban and Sayigh. *The PLO: The Struggle Within* by Alain Gresh[30], and *Revolutionary Transformation in the Arab World* by Walid Kazziha[31] chart the development of groups such as the Democratic Front for the Liberation of Palestine (DFLP) and the Popular Democratic Front for the Liberation of Palestine (PDFLP). They show where the groups came from and their politics, and unwittingly expose why both ended up relying on 'progressive' Arab rulers rather than workers in the region. An absorbing although romanticised account of the training and politics of the guerrilla movement is also provided by Gerard Chaliand in *The Palestinian Resistance.*[32]

The fact that little help was offered to the Palestinian national movement by the region's Communist Parties, even when those parties were extremely influential, is explained by M S Agwani in *Communism in the Arab East.*[33] Dominated by Stalinism, the CPs, particularly those in Egypt and Iraq, were too wrapped up in their national struggle for power, often in alliance with sections of the ruling class, to remember international solidarity with other workers or the Palestinians.

Black September

The inherent contradiction between Fatah's policies of 'mass revolutionary violence' and 'non-interference' exploded in 1970 with tragic consequences. The battle of Karameh in Jordan late in 1968, during which Palestinian guerrillas fought off the might of the Israeli army, inspired thousands more Palestinians to join the PLO and the armed struggle. The region was radicalised by their agitation and example. This was particularly true in Jordan, where Palestinians comprised over two thirds of the population and were supported by most Jordanians, including many in the armed forces. *Green March Black September* by John Cooley describes how the PLO had King Hussein and the Jordanian state in its grasp.[34] It seemed that every family was mobilised and ready to rise up. The left inside the PLO, even many within Fatah, were urging the movement to seize power. Yet the PLO leadership managed to hold them back, declaring that the war was against Israel, not Arab rulers. Abu Daoud, commander of the Palestinian militias in Jordan at the time, said:

> *I was of the opinion that we not only could but should knock off Hussein... Arafat always said 'No'. He told us that making war against Hussein or any Arab regime was not the way to liberation.*[35]

Cooley demonstrates that the inevitable crackdown by King Hussein's loyal troops in September 1970 (Black September) not only led to 3,000 deaths and the unnecessary defeat of a revolution. It also rescued Arafat—by returning the movement to his control. The same tactics, with the same result, were to be repeated time and again. These tactics were best explained by Phil Marshall in this journal:

> *To have confronted the regimes would have meant embracing the idea of change from below, of completely re-orienting the struggle of the mass of Palestinians by linking it directly to the struggles of Arab workers and peasants. This, of course, was never an option — Fatah was never prepared to challenge Arab capitalism, it was committed to acting through the regimes, not toppling them.*[36]

Lebanon

Despite Black September, Fatah remained dominant amongst Palestinians, bolstered by massive funding from Arab rulers. As Tabitha Petran writes: 'Oil states, in particular Saudi Arabia, saw in aid to al-Fatah a means of preserving social peace at home'.[37] The 'responsible' Arafat was courted by governments around the world. A different face was presented to Palestinians. Hart writes, 'If in 1974 Arafat and his senior colleagues had openly admitted the true extent of the compromise they were prepared to make, it and they would have been repudiated and rejected by an easy majority of the Palestinians who were actually engaged in the liberation struggle.'

The focus of that struggle had become Lebanon. In the mid-1970s a left versus right class conflict turned into a long and bloody civil war. Fatah did not disappoint its Arab benefactors in the crucial early period — it refused to intervene. This grim chapter in Palestinian history is covered by several excellent books, the best of which are *Pity the Nation* by *The Independent* journalist Robert Fisk and *The Struggle Over Lebanon* by Tabitha Petran.[38] After years of being bogged down in the civil war, the PLO was finally expelled from Lebanon in 1982 after a prolonged bombardment of Beirut by Israel.[39] Not a single Arab ruler lifted a finger to help it. In the end, Tunis became the distant and almost irrelevant home for a once mighty movement.

The Intifada

Just when the Palestinian nationalist movement seemed dead, the Intifada exploded in the Occupied Territories in December 1987. For the first time since their expulsion, Palestinians took on the Israeli state directly. Within days protests had spread throughout Gaza and the West Bank. Everyone was involved. Youths threw stones. Roads were barricaded. Strikes and boycotts were scrupulously observed. Taxes weren't paid and Palestinian administrators and police resigned. Local committees sprang up and quickly formed the United Command of the Uprising. Each day they produced leaflets and directives, pushing the Intifada forward.

The excitement of the uprising is captured in two books called *Intifada*, one by an American, Don Peretz, the other by two Israeli journalists.[40] However, neither offers much political analysis. This lack is made good by Phil Marshall.[41] Alone among all those covering the uprising, he explains the Intifada in terms of the role played by Zionism and imperialism in the region's history, as well as the failures of Arab nationalism and Stalinism. His descriptions of life in Gaza and the West Bank explain why the Intifada began—and also expose the miserable settlement at Oslo. Over half a million Palestinians live in desperate and cramped poverty in the tiny Gaza Strip. In 1987 Jewish settlers comprised 0.4 percent of the population and had on average 2.6 acres of land. Their Palestinian neighbours had 0.0006 of an acre. The average income in Israel was ten times higher than in Gaza, where the average income is now even lower.[42]

The pain of poverty was compounded by relentless political repression. Independent Palestinian organisations were banned. Every day there were mass arrests, torture and harassment. With no hope of any decisive action from the PLO's Tunis leadership, ordinary Palestinians once more proved that they could not be eliminated, marginalised or forgotten. Marshall shows how the Intifada, although never seriously threatening the Israeli state, rescued the PLO and pushed the Palestinian question back onto the international agenda. The uprising sent shock waves throughout the Middle East. In almost every Arab country, crowds took to the streets in solidarity. Egyptian workers went on strike. Algerians launched their own Intifada. As a result, Arab rulers began panicking. So too did the US, as it watched the stability that guaranteed its cheap oil supplies being undermined.

It was against this background that in 1988 the Palestine National Council, the Palestinian governing body, declared a Palestinian ministate in the Occupied Territories (thereby recognising Israel and accepting a 'two state' solution to the problem). At the same time the US began putting pressure on Israel to come to some agreement that would take the fire out of the Palestinian movement. The long process of negotiations, a product of the Intifada but also a cause of its demise, eventually ended up with the Oslo accords.

Marshall's book offers a complete analysis of the Palestinian nationalist movement, including its left wing, from the 1930s. He shows how none of the organisations were ever free of Arab capital and how none ever made common cause with Arab workers or had the patience to build a revolutionary socialist alternative. His analysis also explains how the failings of the PLO contributed to the rise of Islamic groups during the Intifada, in particular Hamas. This is explored in more detail in *Islamic fundamentalism in the West Bank and Gaza* by Ziad Abu Amr, who shows how the Israeli state originally promoted Hamas as a counterweight to the PLO.[43]

The 'peace process'

When Arafat announced the Oslo peace deal, almost everyone was surprised, especially the Palestinians who had been negotiating in a parallel process in Washington. One man who was not surprised was Mohamed Heikal, a former adviser to Egyptian president Anwar Sadat and a journalist always in the thick of Arab politics. His book *Secret Channels* includes a fascinating account of the diplomacy involved.[44] It is almost embarrassing to read how Rabin and other Israeli leaders treated Arafat, humiliating and tricking him at every turn.

The best book on the peace process, however, is *Palestine in Crisis* by Graham Usher, a socialist journalist who has worked in Gaza for many years.[45] It explains the backdrop, in particular the unstinting US support for Israel, Israel's increasing use of repression after the Intifada, and the bankruptcy of the PLO. By supporting Saddam Hussein in the Gulf War, the PLO lost around $10 billion from the Gulf states in the two years up to the 1993 signing of the Oslo agreement and was in the process of shutting down most of its offices around the world.

Usher highlights the class divisions within the Palestinian nationalist movement and shows the hunger of the PLO leadership to rule, even if only over a token piece of land. In 1993, for example, when violence erupted in Gaza, Arafat responded to what was seen as a challenge to his authority by appointing two of his mates as Fatah's 'sole' leaders in the West Bank and Gaza.

> *Both were from Palestine's landowning elite. The shake-up was widely interpreted to mean that, come the autonomy, it would be the older generation of Palestinian notables who would garner the lion's share of the political spoils, not the younger constituencies of ex-prisoners, workers and students who had come to the fore prior to and during the uprising.*[46]

A few days after signing the Oslo accords, Arafat called on all Palestinians in the Occupied Territories 'to reject violence and terrorism and to return to ordinary life'. From that moment on, Arafat ordered the Fatah Hawks, the organisation's military wing, to manoeuvre for power, using any means necessary against other Palestinians, in preparation for the arrival of 'his' police. Usher reports that since the Palestine National Authority took over, Arafat has spent almost all his 'government's' income on strengthening a police force and intelligence network so that they can do Israel's dirty work. Today they are doing this work with relish, imprisoning and brutalising Palestinians with impunity. Usher also exposes the disastrous tactics of the PFLP and DFLP, who formed an alliance with Hamas, rejected the Oslo deal but then offered nothing as an alternative.

Any lingering doubts anyone may have about the future of the areas under the Palestinian authority are crushed by Usher. They are, he demonstrates, worse than South African bantustans. The economy, including most workers' wages, is almost entirely dependent on Israel—and therefore is devastated when Israel closes its borders, which frequently happens. Ninety percent of citrus fruit grown in Gaza, for instance, ends up in Israeli juice factories. Moreover, the rapid expansion of sub-contracting by Israeli capital to Palestinian entrepreneurs means that ordinary Palestinians are treated like guest workers in their own territory.

The lone Palestinian who has voiced internationally the general despair felt by the masses in Gaza and elsewhere about the 'peace process' is the eloquent writer and academic Edward Said, a long-time resident in the US. His powerful pieces of journalism since the Oslo accords are brought together in *Peace & Its Discontents*.[47] He describes the accords as an 'instrument of capitulation'. He asks what kind of agreement is it that, at the expense of nearly every proclaimed principle of Arab and Palestinian nationalism and struggle, 'has maintained hundreds of Israeli settlements on Palestinian lands, continues to deploy a major army of occupation, intransigently confiscates and builds on Arab land in East Jerusalem and resolutely denies Palestinians true freedom or self-determination.' Said is right to be angry. But he is not entirely blameless for the deal. For many years he was a loyal supporter of Arafat and from 1977 to 1991 was a member of the Palestine National Council. From the 1980s he himself 'surrendered' much of Palestine by advocating a two state solution.

The idea that a Palestinian ministate constructed by imperialism and overshadowed by Israel would satisfy most Palestinians' needs was always a dangerous dream. The idea concedes that the interests of the masses are bound up with their state (and thereby their own ruling classes), and that two peoples, the Jews and the Palestinian Arabs, can never live together in the same country in peace. The two state solution, by definition, denies that there could ever be a democratic, secular state in Palestine where everyone could live together in harmony. Such a solution therefore undermines the struggle of socialists who want to fight for a united Palestine on the basis of class, not nationalist, politics.

The tragedy today is that Palestinians are more isolated than ever from the rest of the Arab working class—the force that could help them realise their aspirations. This isolation is reflected in almost all literature on the Palestinians, which assume that only Palestinians can solve the 'Palestinian problem'. Marshall's book shows how the links with Arab workers could have been, and still should be made, and it is worth looking at books such as *Workers on the Nile* to get a taste of the potential strength of the region's working class.[48] It is time the Palestinians left behind the old politics of nationalism and Stalinism that have failed them so miserably, and began to unite with others in the region who are fighting back against exploitation, oppression and brutal dictators.

Notes

1   People's Press, *Our Roots Are Sill Alive: The Story of the Palestinian People* (Institute for Independent Social Journalism, 1981).
2   D Hirst, *The Gun and the Olive Branch* (Futura, 1977).
3   N Chomsky, *The Fateful Triangle: The United States, Israel and the Palestinians* (Pluto Press, 1983).
4   Ibid, p74.
5   J Rose, *Israel, The Hijack State: America's Watchdog in the Middle East* (Bookmarks, 1986).
6   J Dimbleby and D McCullin, *The Palestinians* (Quartet Books, 1979).

7   E W Said, *The Question of Palestine* (Vintage, 1980); and *The Politics of Dispossession* (Vintage, 1995).

8   D McDowall, *The Palestinians: The Road to Nationhood* (Minority Rights Publications, 1994).

9   N Weinstock, *Zionism: False Messiah* (Ink Links, 1979, revised edition).

10   Two books by Maxime Rodinson also show that the plan for setting up an exclusively Jewish state in Palestine got nowhere until it was taken up by British imperialism—*Israel and the Arabs* (Penguin, 1982) and *Israel: A Colonial-Settler State?* (Pathfinder Press, 1973). Several other excellent books deal with the politics of Zionism. They include *Zionism in the Age of the Dictators* by Lenni Brenner (Croom & Helm, 1983), which also deals with Zionist collaboration with Nazis; *The Other Israel: the Radical Case Against Zionism*, edited by Arie Bober (Anchor Books, 1972), which summarises the policies and politics of Matzpen, the Israeli Socialist Organisation, part of the Fourth International (it eventually collapsed into left wing Zionism); and *Israel: An Apartheid State* by Uri Davis (Zed Books, 1987).

11   S Flapan, *Zionism and the Palestinians* (Croom Helm, 1979).

12   See also H Hanegbi, M Machover, A Orr, *The Class Nature of Israeli Society* (Pluto Press, 1971).

13   P A Smith, *Palestine and Palestinians:1876-1983* (Croom & Helm, 1984).

14   G Kanafani, *Palestine: The 1936-39 Revolt* (unknown).

15   T Hodgkin, *Letters from Palestine 1932-1936* (Quartet Books, 1986).

16   M Budeiri, *The Palestine Communist Party 1919-1948: Arab and Jew in the Struggle for Internationalism* (Ithaca Press, 1979). See also M S Agwami, *Communism in the Arab East* (Asia Publishing House, 1969).

17   See also P Marshall, *Intifada: Zionism, Imperialism and Palestinian Resistance* (Bookmarks, 1989).

18   J Beinin, *Was the Red Flag Flying There?* (I B Taurus, 1990).

19   R Storrs, *Orientations* (Readers Union, 1939).

20   Ibid, p358.

21   R Sayigh, *Palestinians: From Peasants to Revolutionaries* (Zed Press, 1979).

22   W Quandt, F Jabber, A Lesch, *The Politics of Palestinian Nationalism* (University of California Press, 1973).

23   H Cobban, *The Palestinian Liberation Organisation: People, Power and Politics* (Cambridge University Press, 1984).

24   Ibid, p246.

25   See P Marshall, op cit.

26   P Smith, op cit.

27   A Hart, *Arafat: Terrorist of Peacemaker?* (Sidgwick & Jackson, 1984).

28   A Iyad with E Rouleau, *My Home, My Land: A Narrative of the Palestinian Struggle* (Times Books, 1978).

29   See also Abdallah Franji, *The PLO and Palestine* (Zed Books, 1982).

30   A Gresh, *The PLO: The Struggle Within* (Zed Books, 1983).

31   W Kazziha, *Revolutionary Transformation in the Arab World* (Charles Knight & Co, 1975).

32   G Chaliand, *The Palestinian Resistance* (Penguin Books, 1972).

33   M S Agwani, *Communism in the Arab East* (Asia Publishing House, 1969).

34   J K Cooley, *Green March Black September: the Story of the Palestinian Arabs* (Frank Cass, 1973).

35   A Hart, op cit, p304.

36   P Marshall, 'Palestinian nationalism and the Arab revolution', *International Socialism* 2:33, 1986.

37   T Petran, *The Struggle Over Lebanon* (Monthly Review Press, 1987).

38   R Fisk, *Pity the Nation: Lebanon at War* (Oxford University Press, 1991); Petran, op cit; J Randall, *The Tragedy of Lebanon* (Chattus & Windus, 1983). Also useful are H Cobban, *The Making of Modern Lebanon* (Hutchinson, 1985); D Gilmour, *Lebanon: The Fractured Country* (Sphere Books, 1987, Revised editon) and B J Oden, *Lebanon: Dynamics of Conflict* (Zed Books, 1985).

39   See M Jansen, *The Battle of Beirut: Why Israel Invaded Lebanon* (Zed Books, 1982).

40   D Peretz, *Intifada: The Palestinian Uprising* (Westview Press, 1990); and Z Schiff and E Ya'ari, *Intifada* (Touchstone, 1991).

41   P Marshall, *Intifada: Zionism, Imperialism and Palestinian Resistance* (Bookmarks, 1989).

42   Even more detail about living conditions and politics in the Occupied Territories is provided in *Occupation: Israel Over Palestine* (Zed Books, 1984), a compilation of essays by a range of knowledgeable authors; and R Locke and A Stewart, *Bantustan Gaza* (Zed Books, 1985).

43   Z Amr, *Islamic Fundamentalism in the West Bank and Gaza* (Indiana Press University, 1994).

44   M Heikal, *Secret Channels* (Harper Collins, 1996).

45   G Usher, *Palestine in Crisis: The Struggle for Peace and Political Independence After Oslo* (Pluto Press, 1995).

46   Ibid, p16-17.

47   E W Said, *Peace & Its Discontents: Gaza-Jericho 1993-1995* (Vintage, 1995).

48   J Beinin & Z Lockman, *Workers on the Nile: Nationalism, Communism, Islam and the Egyptian Working Class, 1852-1954* (Princeton, 1987). See also E Goldberg, *Tinker, Tailor and Textile Worker: Class and Politics in Egypt, 1930-1952* (Berkeley, 1986) and H Batatu, *The Old Social Classes and the Revolutionary Movements of Iraq* (Princeton, 1978).

The Socialist Workers Party is one of an international grouping of socialist organisations:

AUSTRALIA: International Socialists, GPO Box 1473N, Melbourne 3001

BELGIUM: Socialisme International, Rue Lovinfosse 60, 4030 Grivengée

BRITAIN: Socialist Workers Party, PO Box 82, London E3

CANADA: International Socialists, PO Box 339, Station E, Toronto, Ontario M6H 4E3

CYPRUS: Ergatiki Demokratia, PO Box 7280, Nicosia

DENMARK: Internationale Socialister, Postboks 642, 2200 København N

FRANCE: Socialisme International, BP 189, 75926 Paris Cedex 19

GERMANY: Sozialistische Arbeitergruppe, Postfach 180367, 60084 Frankfurt 1

GREECE: Organosi Sosialisliki Epanastasi, c/o Workers Solidarity, PO Box 8161, Athens 100 10

HOLLAND: International Socialists, PO Box 9720, 3506 GR Utrecht

IRELAND: Socialist Workers Movement, PO Box 1648, Dublin 8

NEW ZEALAND: International Socialist Organization, PO Box 6157, Dunedin

NORWAY: Internasjonale Socialisterr, Postboks 5370, Majorstua, 0304 Oslo 3

POLAND: Solidarność Socjalistyczna, PO Box 12, 01-900 Warszawa 118

SOUTH AFRICA: International Socialists of South Africa, PO Box 18530, Hillbrow 2038, Johannesberg

SPAIN: Socialismo International, Apartardo 563, 08080, Barcelona

UNITED STATES: International Socialist Organisation, PO Box 16085, Chicago, Illinois 60616

ZIMBABWE: International Socialist Organisation, PO Box 6758, Harare

The following issues of *International Socialism* (second series) are available price £3 (including postage) from IS Journal, PO Box 82, London E3 3LH. *International Socialism* 2:58 and 2:65 are available on cassette from the Royal National Institute for the Blind (Peterborough Library Unit). Phone 01733 370777.

International Socialism 2:71 Summer 1996
Chris Harman: The crisis of bourgeois economics ★ Hassan Mahamdallie: William Morris and revolutionary Marxism ★ Alex Callinicos: Darwin, materialism and revolution ★ Chris Nineham: Raymond Williams: revitalising the left? ★ Paul Foot: A passionate prophet of liberation ★ Gill Hubbard: Why has feminism failed women? ★ Lee Sustar: Bookwatch: fighting to unite black and white

International Socialism 2:70 Spring 1996
Alex Callinicos: South Africa after apartheid ★ Chris Harman: France's hot December ★ Brian Richardson: The making of a revolutionary ★ Gareth Jenkins: Why Lucky Jim turned right—an obituary of Kingsley Amis ★ Mark O'Brien: The bloody birth of capitalism ★ Lee Humber: Studies in revolution ★ Adrian Budd: A new life for Lenin ★ Martin Smith: Bookwatch: the General Strike

International Socialism 2:69 Winter 1995
Lindsey German: The Balkan war: can there be peace? ★ Duncan Blackie: The left and the Balkan war ★ Nicolai Gentchev: The myth of welfare dependency ★ Judy Cox: Wealth, poverty and class in Britain today ★ Peter Morgan: Trade unions and strikes ★ Julie Waterson: The party at its peak ★ Megan Trudell: Living to some purpose ★ Nick Howard: The rise and fall of socialism in one city ★ Andy Durgan: Bookwatch: Civil war and revolution in Spain ★

International Socialism 2:68 Autumn 1995
Ruth Brown: Racism and immigration in Britain ★ John Molyneux: Is Marxism deterministic? ★ Stuart Hood: News from nowhere? ★ Lee Sustar: Communism in the heart of the beast ★ Peter Linebaugh: To the teeth and forehead of our faults ★ George Paizis: Back to the future ★ Phil Marshall: The children of stalinism ★ Paul D'Amato: Bookwatch: 100 years of cinema ★

International Socialism 2:67 Summer 1995
Paul Foot: When will the Blair bubble burst? ★ Chris Harman: From Bernstein to Blair—100 years of revisionism ★ Chris Bambery: Was the Second World War a war for democracy? ★ Chris Nineham: Is the media all powerful? ★ Peter Morgan: How the West was won ★ Charlie Hore: Bookwatch: China since Mao ★

International Socialism 2:66 Spring 1995
Dave Crouch: The crisis in Russia and the rise of the right ★ Phil Gasper: Cruel and unusual punishment: the politics of crime in the United States ★ Alex Callinicos: Backwards to liberalism ★ John Newsinger: Matewan: film and working class struggle ★ John Rees: the light and the dark ★ Judy Cox: how to make the Tories disappear ★ Charlie Hore: Jazz: a reply to the critics ★ Pat Riordan: Bookwatch: Ireland ★

International Socialism 2:65 Special issue
Lindsey German: Frederick Engels: life of a revolutionary ★ John Rees: Engels' Marxism ★ Chris Harman: Engels and the origins of human society ★ Paul McGarr: Engels and natural science ★

International Socialism 2:64 Autumn 1994
Chris Harman: The prophet and the proletariat ★ Kieran Allen: What is changing in Ireland ★ Mike Haynes: The wrong road on Russia ★ Rob Ferguson: Hero and villain ★ Jane Elderton: Suffragette style ★ Chris Nineham: Two faces of modernism ★ Mike Hobart, Dave Harker and Matt Kelly: Three replies to 'Jazz—a people's music?' ★ Charlie Kimber: Bookwatch: South Africa—the struggle continues ★

International Socialism 2:63 Summer 1994
Alex Callinicos: Crisis and class struggle in Europe today ★ Duncan Blackie: The United Nations and the politics of imperialism ★ Brian Manning: The English Revolution and the transition from feudalism to capitalism ★ Lee Sustar: The roots of multi-racial labour unity in the United States

★ Peter Linebaugh: Days of villainy: a reply to two critics ★ Dave Sherry: Trotsky's last, greatest struggle ★ Peter Morgan: Geronimo and the end of the Indian wars ★ Dave Beecham: Ignazio Silone and *Fontamara* ★ Chris Bambery: Bookwatch: understanding fascism ★

International Socialism 2:62 Spring 1994
Sharon Smith: Mistaken identity—or can identity politics liberate the oppressed? ★ Iain Ferguson: Containing the crisis—crime and the Tories ★ John Newsinger: Orwell and the Spanish Revolution ★ Chris Harman: Change at the first millenium ★ Adrian Budd: Nation and empire—Labour's foreign policy 1945-51 ★ Gareth Jenkins: Novel questions ★ Judy Cox: Blake's revolution ★ Derek Howl: Bookwatch: the Russian Revolution ★

International Socialism 2:61 Winter 1994
Lindsey German: Before the flood? ★ John Molyneux: The 'politically correct' controversy ★ David McNally: E P Thompson—class struggle and historical materialism ★ Charlie Hore: Jazz—a people's music ★ Donny Gluckstein: Revolution and the challenge of labour ★ Charlie Kimber: Bookwatch: the Labour Party in decline ★

International Socialism 2:60 Autumn 1993
Chris Bambery: Euro-fascism: the lessons of the past and present tasks ★ Chris Harman: Where is capitalism going? (part 2) ★ Mike Gonzalez: Chile and the struggle for workers' power ★ Phil Marshall: Bookwatch: Islamic activism in the Middle East ★

International Socialism 2:59 Summer 1993
Ann Rogers: Back to the workhouse ★ Kevin Corr and Andy Brown: The labour aristocracy and the roots of reformism ★ Brian Manning: God, Hill and Marx ★ Henry Maitles: Cutting the wire: a criticial appraisal of Primo Levi ★ Hazel Croft: Bookwatch: women and work ★

International Socialism 2:58 Spring 1993
Chris Harman: Where is capitalism going? (part one) ★ Ruth Brown and Peter Morgan: Politics and the class struggle today: a roundtable discussion ★ Richard Greeman: The return of Comrade Tulayev: Victor Serge and the tragic vision of Stalinism ★ Norah Carlin: A new English revolution ★ John Charlton: Building a new world ★ Colin Barker: A reply to Dave McNally ★

International Socialism 2:57 Winter 1992
Lindsey German: Can there be a revolution in Britain? ★ Mike Haynes: Columbus, the Americas and the rise of capitalism ★ Mike Gonzalez: The myths of Columbus: a history ★ Paul Foot: Poetry and revolution ★ Alex Callinicos: Rhetoric which cannot conceal a bankrupt theory: a reply to Ernest Mandel ★ Charlie Kimber: Capitalism, cruelty and conquest ★ David McNulty: Comments on Colin Barker's review of Thompson's *Customs in Common* ★

International Socialism 2:56 Autumn 1992
Chris Harman: The Return of the National Question ★ Dave Treece: Why the Earth Summit failed ★ Mike Gonzalez: Can Castro survive? ★ Lee Humber and John Rees: The good old cause—an interview with Christopher Hill ★ Ernest Mandel: The Impasse of Schematic Dogmatism ★

International Socialism 2:55 Summer 1992
Alex Callinicos: Race and class ★ Lee Sustar: Racism and class struggle in the American Civil War era ★ Lindsey German and Peter Morgan: Prospects for socialists—an interview with Tony Cliff ★ Robert Service: Did Lenin lead to Stalin? ★ Samuel Farber: In defence of democratic revolutionary socialism ★ David Finkel: Defending 'October' or sectarian dogmatism? ★ Robin Blackburn: Reply to John Rees ★ John Rees: Dedicated followers of fashion ★ Colin Barker: In praise of custom ★ Sheila McGregor: Revolutionary witness ★

International Socialism 2:54 Spring 1992
Sharon Smith: Twilight of the American dream ★ Mike Haynes: Class and crisis—the transition in eastern Europe ★ Costas Kossis: A miracle without end? Japanese capitalism and the world economy ★ Alex Callinicos: Capitalism and the state system: A reply to Nigel Harris ★ Steven Rose: Do animals have rights? ★ John Charlton: Crime and class in the 18th century ★ John Rees: Revolution, reform and working class culture ★ Chris Harman: Blood simple ★

International Socialism 2:52 Autumn 1991
John Rees: In defence of October ★ Ian Taylor and Julie Waterson: The political crisis in Greece—an interview with Maria Styllou and Panos Garganas ★ Paul McGarr: Mozart, overture to revolution ★ Lee Humber: Class, class consciousness and the English Revolution ★ Derek Howl: The legacy of Hal Draper ★

International Socialism 2:51 Summer 1991
Chris Harman: The state and capitalism today ★ Alex Callinicos: The end of nationalism? ★ Sharon Smith: Feminists for a strong state? ★ Colin Sparks and Sue Cockerill: Goodbye to the Swedish miracle ★ Simon Phillips: The South African Communist Party and the South African working class ★ John Brown: Class conflict and the crisis of feudalism ★

International Socialism 2:49 Winter 1990
Chris Bambery: The decline of the Western Communist Parties ★ Ernest Mandel: A theory which has not withstood the test of time ★ Chris Harman: Criticism which does not withstand the test of logic ★ Derek Howl: The law of value In the USSR ★ Terry Eagleton: Shakespeare and the class struggle ★ Lionel Sims: Rape and pre-state societies ★ Sheila McGregor: A reply to Lionel Sims ★

International Socialism 2:48 Autumn 1990
Lindsey German: The last days of Thatcher ★ John Rees: The new imperialism ★ Neil Davidson and Donny Gluckstein: Nationalism and the class struggle in Scotland ★ Paul McGarr: Order out of chaos ★

International Socialism 2:46 Winter 1989
Chris Harman: The storm breaks ★ Alex Callinicos: Can South Africa be reformed? ★ John Saville: Britain, the Marshall Plan and the Cold War ★ Sue Clegg: Against the stream ★ John Rees: The rising bourgeoisie ★

International Socialism 2:44 Autumn 1989
Charlie Hore: China: Tiananmen Square and after ★ Sue Clegg: Thatcher and the welfare state ★ John Molyneux: *Animal Farm* revisited ★ David Finkel: After Arias, is the revolution over? ★ John Rose: Jews in Poland ★

International Socialism 2:43 Summer 1989 (Reprint—special price £4.50)
Marxism and the Great French Revolution by Paul McGarr and Alex Callinicos

International Socialism 2:42 Spring 1989
Chris Harman: The myth of market socialism ★ Norah Carlin: Roots of gay oppression ★ Duncan Blackie: Revolution in science ★ International Socialism Index ★

International Socialism 2:41 Winter 1988
Polish socialists speak out: Solidarity at the Crossroads ★ Mike Haynes: Nightmares of the market ★ Jack Robertson: Socialists and the unions ★ Andy Strouthous: Are the unions in decline? ★ Richard Bradbury: What is Post-Structuralism? ★ Colin Sparks: George Bernard Shaw ★

International Socialism 2:39 Summer 1988
Chris Harman and Andy Zebrowski: Glasnost, before the storm ★ Chanie Rosenberg: Labour and the fight against fascism ★ Mike Gonzalez: Central America after the Peace Plan ★ Ian Birchall: Raymond Williams ★ Alex Callinicos: Reply to John Rees ★

International Socialism 2:35 Summer 1987
Pete Green: Capitalism and the Thatcher years ★ Alex Callinicos: Imperialism, capitalism and the state today ★ Ian Birchall: Five years of *New Socialist* ★ Callinicos and Wood debate 'Looking for alternatives to reformism' ★ David Widgery replies on 'Beating Time' ★

International Socialism 2:31 Winter 1985
Alex Callinicos: Marxism and revolution In South Africa ★ Tony Cliff: The tragedy of A J Cook ★ Nigel Harris: What to do with London? The strategies of the GLC ★

International Socialism 2:30 Autumn 1985
Gareth Jenkins: Where is the Labour Party heading? ★ David McNally: Debt, inflation and the rate of profit ★ Ian Birchall: The terminal crisis in the British Communist Party ★ replies on Women's oppression and *Marxism Today* ★

International Socialism 2:25 Autumn 1984
John Newsinger: Jim Larkin, Syndicalism and the 1913 Dublin Lockout ★ Pete Binns: Revolution and state capitalism in the Third World ★ Colin Sparks: Towards a police state? ★ Dave Lyddon: Demystifying the downturn ★ John Molyneux: Do working class men benefit from women's oppression? ★

International Socialism 2:18 Winter 1983
Donny Gluckstein: Workers' councils in Western Europe ★ Jane Ure Smith: The early Communist press in Britain ★ John Newsinger: The Bolivian Revolution ★ Andy Durgan: Largo Caballero and Spanish socialism ★ M Barker and A Beezer: Scarman and the language of racism ★

International Socialism 2:14 Winter 1981
Chris Harman: The riots of 1981 ★ Dave Beecham: Class struggle under the Tories ★ Tony Cliff: Alexandra Kollontai ★ L James and A Paczuska: Socialism needs feminism ★ reply to Cliff on Zetkin ★ Feminists In the labour movement ★

International Socialism 2:13 Summer 1981
Chris Harman: The crisis last time ★ Tony Cliff: Clara Zetkin ★ Ian Birchall: Left Social Democracy In the French Popular Front ★ Pete Green: Alternative Economic Strategy ★ Tim Potter: The death of Eurocommunism ★

International Socialism 2:12 Spring 1981
Jonathan Neale: The Afghan tragedy ★ Lindsey German: Theories of patriarchy ★ Ray Challinor: McDouall and Physical Force Chartism ★ S Freeman & B Vandesteeg: Unproductive labour ★ Alex Callinicos: Wage labour and capitalism ★ Italian fascism ★ Marx's theory of history ★ Cabral ★